SISTER
RESISTERS

SISTER RESISTERS

Mentoring Black Women on Campus

Janie Victoria Ward and Tracy L. Robinson-Wood

Harvard Education Press
Cambridge, MA

Paperback ISBN 978-1-68253-722-0

Library of Congress Cataloging-in-Publication Data is on file.

Published by Harvard Education Press,
an imprint of the Harvard Education Publishing Group

Harvard Education Press
8 Story Street
Cambridge, MA 02138

Cover Design: Endpaper Studio
Cover Image: AtlasbyAtlas Studio/Shutterstock.com

The typefaces in this book are ITC Legacy Sans, ITC Legacy Serif, Myriad Pro, and Minion Pro

CONTENTS

We dedicate this book to our precious ancestors and to all the unborn spirits who have yet to join us. Because of you, we envision a brighter and more hopeful world.

PREFACE

"THE BEAUTIFUL THING ABOUT LEARNING is nobody can take it away from you."[1] For generations, Black parents have impressed upon their children the belief that education is the great equalizer. Internalizing this message of Black empowerment and social mobility, Black students have long sought access to postsecondary education. Up until the 1960s, most Black students were enrolled in historically Black colleges and universities. By the 1970s, enrollment patterns began to shift, and with the onset of federal grant programs primarily aimed at low-income students, the presence and impact of Black students on predominantly White college campuses became more significant. The doors of opportunity in White colleges opened for Black populations and many others. Growing numbers of students from previously marginalized groups entered college and their attendance contributed to the diversity we now see in our higher education institutions.

Over the past two decades there has been an increase in college enrollment rates among eighteen- to twenty-four-year-olds who are Black, Latinx, and White. This news is encouraging for Black college students in general. However, the numbers of Black women in college today are not that different statistically than they looked twenty years ago.[2]

Black women who are represented in college enrollment data include traditional-age Black female college students and, increasingly non-traditional-age Black women, often called *adult learners*. Many of these women are newly attending college, while others are returning to college to finish their degree.[3] Together, these students bring to campus a wide range of academic aspirations, challenges, and life experiences that are discussed in this book.

Race and economics are important factors in determining where students attend college. More specifically, the percentage of undergraduate students at private for-profit four-year institutions who are Black is more than double the percentages of Black students at private nonprofit and public four-year institutions. For-profit institutions often aggressively market themselves to potential students as more accessible, offering flexible degree programs (often online) that purportedly address the needs of working students. Such advertisements are alluring to disproportionately non-traditional-college-aged Black women with children.[4] These schools tend to be more expensive, and research shows that students leave with higher debt obligations, fewer transferable credits, and less earning potential following graduation.[5] The recent 2020 pandemic and the deregulation of for-profit institutions has created a resurgence in this sector of higher education. Given their intensive recruitment practices, there is no doubt many more Black students will continue to enroll.[6] Although there could be overlaps, we suspect that the mentoring of Black students in these for-profit schools may look different than mentoring in two- and four-year public and private institutions, which is the primary focus of our book.

Significant differences in social class, ethnic background, language, national origin, sexuality, geographic location, and religious orientation exist among Black women in college. Such diversity contributes to a wide range of experiences for students studying in person, as well as for those learning remotely. Research examining the experiences of Black students in higher education is extensive, but one primary consensus appears to emerge in these studies. Black students confront a host of discriminatory attitudes, practices, and behaviors in college settings. How students respond to these stressors can promote or disrupt successful degree completion. This book provides a way of understanding the specific challenges faced by Black women as their experiences sit at the intersection of racial and gender bias. By bringing their unique experiences to light, we highlight the supports that we feel these women need to successfully negotiate the inequities they face.

We adopt a developmental approach to understanding the needs of Black college women. Years earlier, when in high school, some young

Black women had access to the guidance they needed to prepare for life after secondary school. But unfortunately, many Black students did not. Depending on where students attended high school, teachers, school nurses, and counselors may have been there to answer questions and offer advice. Making the transition from high school to college life is disorienting. School support staff know that college can be a completely alien context to master. Once students arrive at college, the availability of resources may seem overwhelming. Some students may not have the skills to adequately assess their needs, yet colleges often expect otherwise. We assume that they will engage in complex problem-solving and will make mature decisions on their own. We anticipate that young people will coalesce all of the lessons learned in childhood and adolescence to build healthy, sustainable lives for themselves and subsequently for their offspring. This is the traditional path to independence. For some, the roadway is and has always been clear. For other students, potholes and pitfalls litter the walkway, and their successful passage is far less certain.

In general, Black women in the US have fewer supports to turn to outside of family and friends. At the same time, the vulnerabilities associated with managing the responsibilities of adulthood loom large. Unfortunately for these women, the consequences of missteps are at their highest during this period. Poor choices have long-term consequences with respect to health, safety, income maintenance, and, of course, college completion.

This book translates what we have learned about promoting college retention and applying this knowledge specifically to Black female students. A number of books have been written about this population and, like ours, they focus on the impact of bias and discrimination on students' racial and gender identities and its bearing on college success.[7] And there are several books that look at mentoring practices and students of color.[8]

Our analysis goes a step further. In these pages, we explore the many ways in which biased attitudes and discriminatory behaviors surface in the daily lives of Black women in college. We identify circumstances that call for resistance responses, and we analyze what that resistance could or should look like and why. Finally, we center this work in our model of cross-racial mentoring in higher education, a practice that calls for a very intentional focus on developing resistance skills in both Black mentees and the adult mentors (who are often White women) working with them.

The impetus for this *Sister Resisters* book started over three decades ago. We began mapping the initial contours of our theory of resistance in a 1991 article, "'A Belief in Self Far Greater than Anyone's Disbelief.'"[9] This elegant axiom was originally written by the Black playwright August Wilson, and this distinctive wisdom became our touchstone. The forcefulness of its truth energized us. Over the years, we gave presentations on the role of resistance in the lives of Black girls and women, and our work was met with great interest at professional conferences, in schools, and at community-based organizations. Often, Black people and other people of color would share their own stories of personal and collective resistance at the end of our talks. They thanked us for drawing on the strengths of Black folks' cultural knowledge. Black mothers, teachers, and clinicians, in particular, felt that the lessons of resistance to oppression that they had learned and passed on to their own children were finally validated by professionals in the field. White educators at these presentations shared stories with us too. They had seen the academic success of too many smart Black students interrupted by poor choices emanating from emotional distress. They personally knew black students who were overcome by self-doubt and "racial battle fatigue."[10] These White educators, lingering behind after the workshops, seemed to eavesdrop on the conversations we were having with the people of color. They wanted to learn more about what we meant by *resistance*—its history, relevance, and application for Black youth development. Most of all, they wanted to know how they, like the mothers and teachers they were listening to, could join with us in Black students' resistance.

As the years went on, we continued to refine our ideas. We published books and multiple research articles that further defined and mapped resistance for Black women in adolescence and during adulthood. As university professors, our access to Black, Indigenous, and People of Color (BIPOC) women completing their undergraduate and graduate degrees afforded us opportunities to review and revise our notions of resistance, particularly as they operated within the uneven power dynamics of higher education institutions. The young women on our research teams, in our classes, and in our focus groups shared a wealth of information about how they were interpreting their life chal-lenges on and off campus. They expanded our understanding of the sociopolitical world from their native/indigenous perspectives as Black millennials and Gen Zers in ways that have been immeasurably valu-able. In these meetings, we heard the connections young women were making across their social identities. We translated our notions of resis-tance and established their cultural relevance for Black girls and women and for other groups who also contend with multiple layers of societal oppression. The work of developing one's ability to *withstand* negative social influences while *taking a stand* for self-validation and group affir-mation led us to the thesis of this book.

Resistance can be put in motion by an individual, and it can be activated by the collective. Traditionally, Black Americans have resisted their oppression largely alone, or at times with the help of other Black individuals or associations, but there is a long history in this nation of White allyship. White individuals, challenging the status quo, have stood up to racism and joined Black people in the struggle for social jus-tice and civil rights.[11] We write this book in the spirit of all people across racial classifications who reject racism. We acknowledge the devastating toll racial discrimination has had on all of humanity, its destruction of Black families and communities, and its thwarting of Black social prog-ress. The resistance we share is a fulfillment of our ancestors' struggles, a commitment to the present, and our promise to future generations.

There are countless Black college-age women who may need assis-tance from the caring adults in our colleges. They need help to push back against invalidating individuals and systems that misunderstand their needs or do not have their best interests at heart. These are the Sister Resisters on whom we call to enter the circle.

Uses of Language

It is important to take a moment to speak to the language choices that we have made in this book as they relate to race and gender. Today, the terminology used to describe people of African descent is as varied as we are. *Black, African American, people of color,* and more recently *BIPOC* are undoubtedly familiar terms. Some authors use *Black* and *African Ameri-can* interchangeably, and at times in this text we do as well. Although we realize this practice is contested, we prefer to capitalize both Black and White when referring to groups in racial, ethnic, or cultural terms as it conveys a shared sense of identity and history. We see Black and White both as historically created racial identities, and "grammatical justice" would instruct that whatever rule applies to one should apply to the other.[12] We acknowledge and respect the strong feelings about self-identification held by many individuals. We hope that our racial (and gender) terminology is inclusive and representative of the ways people self-define, particularly those with marginalized identities.

When we reference people who are Black, we are referring to Blackness on multiple levels. First, the term Black serves as a phenotypic marker that has historically targeted certain bodies for discriminatory behavior in the US and in many other societies in the Western world. Blackness also speaks to a social and political identification with a group of people who share a sense of culture, who have knowledge of their histories of resistance to oppression across time and space, and who racially identify as Black. Blackness also includes a source and sense of belonging.

Among people of African descent, specific references to nationality, geography, and ethnicity are sometimes preferred. In these cases, we will use such identifications as needed. We also recognize that many people on our college campuses identify as biracial and/or multiracial. Thus, a binary focus on racial identity can feel limiting for these individuals. Moreover, the suggestion of a racial binary is problematic. It is exclusionary and it is an inaccurate reflection of the reality of biracial and multiracial people's intrapsychic realities and lived experiences. We hope that multiracial individuals, particularly those with African ancestry, will find their needs and concerns reflected in these pages, even when their complex racial identities are not specifically named.

Gender terminology too has exploded in recent years. We are aware that the field is fluid, and in these pages we have tried to stay informed of the additions and edits to gender language use, particularly as it pertains to Black college women. Biases exist across multiple identities and proffer that certain bodies are preferred over others. Through our analysis, writing, and case studies, we endeavor to make evident our opposition to gender as a fixed and uncomplicated binary.

Cis-sexism, the preferential treatment of cisgender persons (those whose sex assigned at birth aligns with their gender identity) is too often coupled with discrimination against transgender, third-gender, and genderqueer people.[13] We reject the implicit (and in some cases explicit) assumption that cisgender is the preferred or correct way of being.[14]

When we reference gender, we seek to be inclusive of the affectional orientation and gender identities that include diverse sexualities and genders, marginalized orientations, and intersex individuals.[15] At times, we specifically use the terms *queer* and *gender nonconforming* to recognize the particular histories, struggles, and commitments of people who challenge gender boundaries to fully reflect their identities.[16] We also adopt the nonbinary pronouns *they*, *them*, and *theirs* in our case studies as many people find pronouns to be an important affirmation of identity. We believe that respecting someone's sense of authentic identity, including using their pronouns and chosen name, is a basic human courtesy.

References to White Women

Women who are "White" represent the majority of professionals in student affairs and related careers, particularly in predominantly White institutions. In the discussion that follows, we move away from the traditional association of people and their pigmentation as fixed and immutable categories. Hence, our use of the term *White* is mindful of how the concept refers to the multiple social advantages conferred on individuals of White European descent.

As race scholar Ibram Kendi writes, "Anti-racism demands that we identify racially in order to identify the privileges (and disadvantages) we possess."[17] Here, we acknowledge the tension of noting that race is a social construct, even as it has an autonomous and pervasive life of its own in our society. White women are not a monolithic group. As members of this society, they, like everyone else, possess intersectional social identities across multiple domains. We invite mentors, who are most often White women, to explore their individual identity statuses that may overlap with stigmatized identities—for example, having a disability, identifying as lesbian, gay, bisexual, transgender, intersex, and/or queer (LGBTIQ), coming from a low-income earning class structure, and being a member of a religious minority. There is much to be learned by interrogating why these intersectional connections may matter across contexts. Knowledge can be gained from understanding how the advantages and disadvantages evoked from these different social identities affect relationships across social differences.

While we refer to White women as a group, it is not our intention to overgeneralize and essentialize White women. Moreover, we respect that historically, some White women have been interrogating their proximity to racism, inclusion, and privilege. Race dialogues, White affinity study groups, and experiential seminars represent an array of opportunities available to White people interested in understanding race, racism, and who they are as racial beings. The concepts, stories, and case studies presented in this book are intended to resonate with a diversity of college personnel across multiple identities. These stories may remind you of the students you have taught, situations you have faced, and race-based dilemmas you have navigated in your professional lives. And they may provide answers to questions you may have about race, identity, and education.

Reframing Resistance

In the field of psychology, *resistance* generally invokes a negative connotation as it is a term often applied to a patient's lack of cooperation or refusal to comply with a treatment plan. The field of education often refers to *resistance* when describing a student's refusal to engage with school. Although resistance for educators can be subtle or overt, it is usually associated with oppositional, disruptive, and belligerent behavior, suggesting something that needs to be reduced or eliminated for positive outcomes to occur.

In this book, we assign a different meaning to *resistance*. First and foremost, we position individual and collective pushback against systems of domination that exist on multiple levels: psychological, social, political, and economic. Our understanding of resistance emerges from the knowledge acquired over the years by African American people living under conditions of racial inequality. Resistance reflects the enduring power of a people whose liberatory strength has maintained and sustained survival and actively challenges dehumanization brought on by chronic oppression. When we speak here of Black people's power, we are not "drawing a false equivalence to the concept of racial superiority espoused by the white power movement."[18] We rebuke a power whose purpose is to thieve, abuse, and destroy. Instead, we deliberately name and call forth *resistance*, as the power that has allowed Black people to rise up, transform, love, heal, and move forward. And it is this life force that can be harnessed for all people whose lives are constrained by the weight of oppression.

Given that White people are in the majority as staff and faculty members on predominantly White campuses, we devote a great deal of attention to the development of White women as Sister Resisters. Increasingly, Black women, Indigenous women, and women of color are employed as faculty and staff in higher education institutions. These women may also function as mentors and bring their own cultural histories to the work of mentoring. Our template for Sister Resisters is embedded in Black women's ways of knowing, decision-making, and navigation of gendered racism. We acknowledge that other women of color, and some Black women, may be at varying levels of awareness regarding resistance. And not all forms of resistance help women to live their best lives. We believe there is much in this book for all Sister Resisters to explore for their own and for their mentees' empowerment.

In 1991, we first introduced our theory of resistance for Black girls and women. In the introduction, we discuss the history of that theory and our motivations for writing this provocative book, and we share the heuristic traditions that inform our ideas. In this preface we continue our discussion of resistance as laying the groundwork for our Sister Resister mentoring model. Our focus is on White women who represent the majority of staff and faculty at predominantly White colleges and universities and will most likely mentor Black female college students. We highlight the key features in this work: the intentionality of mentoring relationships, the role of power dynamics, the integration of life span developmental perspectives, and the importance of intersectionality. Moreover, the introduction addresses the reciprocal development of cross-racial pairings between Black mentees and White mentors.

In chapter 1, we expand upon our theory of resistance—namely, its meaning, intent, and purpose. We introduce our Sister Resister mentoring model and describe its relevance for mentoring Black female college students today. We review the research literature regarding Black students' college experiences, examining campus climates and especially microaggressions, gendered racial stereotypes, and the negotiation of race inside the classroom and across campus. We explore the dual forces of development, arguing that during this time of tremendous change and upheaval, identity is unfolding within an environment that is far too often invalidating and insensitive to the needs of Black female college students. We conclude this chapter with a discussion of optimal and suboptimal resistance—affect, action, and awareness, which sets the stage for the application of resistance theory relative to women's lives.

In chapter 2, we pivot from a discussion of Black students to the White women who may become their mentors. We discuss the potential barriers to the mentoring relationship by examining how the normativity of Whiteness can adversely impact relational connection. The relevance of resistance for White women is explored through our interrogation of patriarchy and of White supremacist beliefs that exert authority on Black and White women, separately and together. We identify what White women need to know in order to resist the consequences of women's gender oppression. Sociopolitical knowledge that informs White mentors' self-awareness, as well as the knowledge they need to understand Black women's experiences with the intersecting and compounding effects of racial and gender oppression, is examined. The complicated dynamics of developing relational trust within cross-racial relationships are explored.

Our third chapter turns to Sister Resisters and the work of meaningful mentoring. Sister Resisters refers to White female mentors working intentionally in deep and meaningful relationships with Black female students. Although BIPOC women can be and often are Sister Resisters for Black college women, this book focuses on White women who are in the majority at predominantly white institutions. There we discuss the meaning of *reciprocal development*, referring to the racialized knowledge about racial realities that the junior mentee introduces to the relationship, which may surpass that of her White mentor. Understanding the mentoring space within the Sister Resister model is also discussed. This speaks to the skills and talents White mentors bring to the relationship that can become a dynamic catalyst for Black female students' personal and academic development, particularly when the mentor is culturally knowledgeable, engaged, and purposeful. The meaning and importance of calling out institutional racism is also covered, as is the application of resistance to both women's everyday lives.

Due to the centrality of relationships in the lives of Black women navigating predominantly White college spaces, our attention in chapter 4 is focused on what Black students say they need and desire when making strong relational connections. Black women's sisterhood is presented. On the other hand, sometimes Black women's relationships with other Black women can lead to conflict due to differences within race and across ethnicity and class. We discuss Black and White women's relationships and explicate the meaning of reconstituting cross-racial relationships that are in the service of healthy resistance. The significance of mentors' honest and validating conversations with mentees particularly about race and racism is a central theme discussed in this chapter and throughout the book. We acknowledge that such conversations can be difficult for women, yet we argue that strong, meaningful, and productive cross-racial mentoring relationships are dependent upon this commitment.

In chapter 5, we discuss the complexities of cultural mistrust within Black and White women's relationships. By understanding the historical roots of these relational disconnections, we explore how women's relationships (both inter- and intraracial) have been used to uphold patriarchy, racism, and other power inequities in the United States. Case studies in this chapter explore how oppressive forces shape institutional curriculum and policies. There is a need for Sister Resisters to respond to institutional practices that impede Black college women's progress, and sometimes this can be done with the support of adult peer mentors. Suboptimal resistance is defined, and the uses of power and privilege are examined as dynamic features that require attention in cross-racial mentoring relationships. Supporting the resistance responses of Black female students can be challenging for both mentors and mentees. Because mentors may be called upon to negotiate this work in less than favorable environments, we discuss the role of courage and perseverance as fundamental to the sustainability of healthy resistance relationships.

In our sixth and final chapter, we present tools for resistance, including decision-making capacities and problem-solving techniques, emotional intelligence to handle race-based affect and resolve race-based conflicts, a strong self-concept, racial self-efficacy, sociopolitical awareness, cultural knowledge, and self-advocacy. We map these skills onto our four-dimensional model: see it, name it, oppose it, and replace it. The prowess of resistance to energize Black women mentees and their mentors echoes through this final chapter and has special relevance within the context of mental health. The economic, psychological, and social disruptions brought on by the worldwide pandemic and the structural inequalities that preceded and worsened during the coronavirus crisis have intensified Black students' mental health needs. We end the final chapter by shedding light on the importance of self-care and allyship in order to do the work of mentoring and resistance. We follow chapter 6 with a list of recommendations that summarize essential tools for staying true to the Sister Resister model.

Now, let's begin with reflections upon our own mentoring experiences.

Janie's Mentoring Experiences

When I attended college in the mid-1970s, there was very little mention of mentoring programs designed for my age group. Mentoring was something that adults (usually men) did after they finished college and were navigating their professional climb up the corporate ladder. Few educators spoke of mentoring as a needed service that colleges had a responsibility to provide to all of their students.

Beginning in the late 1960s, Black and other non-White students entered predominantly White institutions in numbers greater than ever before. The descriptive term we use today, *first-generation students*, had not yet been coined, and from a student's perspective, I don't remember hearing much institutional chatter about what postsecondary education should be doing to meet our specific needs. I attended a tiny, race and economically diverse, progressive hippy high school, with a total population of seventy-two students when everyone bothered to show up. Except for a handful of full-pay families, the kids of color who attended were working class or low income. Many of my White classmates, on the other hand, were the children of local university professors, doctors, lawyers, and other professionals. Some were even "legacy kids" whose families had college campus buildings named after them. Despite our economic differences, nearly all of my friends in the diverse group I hung out with were headed to college. Where I grew up in 1973, a postsecondary education after high school was a given. Colleges were expanding, financial aid was plentiful, and, across the nation, the rush was on to diversify college campuses.

I was eighteen years old when I began an accelerated program at Boston University (BU) as a commuter student to lessen the financial burden of that first academic degree. I had very few decisions to make in that program; the curriculum was predetermined, as was the timetable of when the courses were scheduled. I volunteered on weekends at the local public television station, and though I knew it was an unusual aspiration for a nineteen-year-old Black girl, I wanted to become a television director. I loved hanging out in the production control room, with its video switches, mixing consoles, and a director who was large and in charge. The work was tension filled, but creative nonetheless, and only a few people had the technical skills to do it well. I wanted to be one of those people, and after my sophomore year at BU, I decided to transfer to New York University's film school and follow my dream.

My confidence began to crumble on day one, when for the first time I felt what it meant to be a "first-gen." The university was huge and confusing, and as a transfer student I had to work my way through its systems largely alone. Lots of other things were unfamiliar too. Living in Manhattan is very different from living in Boston; courses in an art school curriculum are nothing like the prescribed humanities courses I had aced at BU, and professional preparation for a highly competitive, cutthroat career in the entertainment industry was nothing like anything I had known or experienced in my life to date. Although I didn't know it then, I know now that having a mentor undoubtedly would have helped.

No one I grew up with knew the entertainment business, and I knew little about how my race and my gender would hold me back in the field. While volunteering in public TV, I met maybe one or two Black people in the industry: photographers, audio engineers, and cameramen. I can't recall any women behind the camera or in the production studio. Black women who looked like me were nowhere to be found. Many of my White college classmates, on the other hand, had relatives, family friends, or other contacts in the field. They formed their cliques, and I was not in them. The students in my classes showed no inclination to be inclusive, and they expressed no desire to introduce an outsider into what was then an expanding, albeit highly competitive, field. It was more of a quiet, unarticulated cutthroat competitiveness, one I was neither used to nor knew how to navigate. Unclear about the barriers before me, I didn't understand how to deal with being so Black and so female in a lily-white man's profession. Nothing had prepared me for making this leap in life, and rather than risk failure, I slowly abandoned my plans for a career in the industry. I regret to this day being so unschooled about structural racism and sexism and thus unprepared for the professional world. Would a mentor have kept me in the field? Could she have listened to my poorly articulated observations and complaints, and guided me through the unwritten rules in play? Where might I have been today had I received the specialized support and encouragement my unique journey had required? Facing those career decisions as an anxious Black undergraduate with little knowledge of what breaking into the industry would demand of me was frightening and frustrating, and enough to make me abandon my dream.

Graduate school was a different adventure altogether. By then, mentoring had become popular outside of corporate America and I was surrounded by savvy students zealously scouring faculty lists in search of a perfect match. I knew enough to watch what my classmates were doing, but again, there were fewer candid conversations about our postgraduation plans than I expected and desperately needed. At least, that was the case with my White classmates.

My Black and Brown classmates, on the other hand, were eager to break the silences. We'd share what we knew with each other, including our past experiences and our future dreams. Among my Black friends, race and gender were central to nearly all of our conversations. We heatedly debated the invisibility of racial perspectives in the curriculum. We identified how structural racism upheld ideological frameworks within the disciplines we studied. Indeed, the anger we felt about our exclusion in social theory and the deficit framings of racialized minorities in practice was what drew us into graduate school in the first place. Those conversations with my Black colleagues shaped me; they nurtured my research interests and strengthened my determination to become a change agent in the field of developmental science.

I would have been lost in the absence of the intellectual anchoring and culturally relevant peer mentoring offered by my BIPOC sisters and brothers in graduate school. But their contribution didn't meet all of my preprofessional needs. When it came time to job hunt, my professors offered encouragement, but with very little advice.

It was a tough job market for new academics in the late 1980s, and I was clueless about seeking out an institution best matched to my needs. Should I apply to work at a college or a university? Public or private? School of education or traditional psychology department? Most importantly, I had no idea how, during a job interview, to suss out the *truth* about an institution's racial climate—that is, how the college was really experienced by its Black students, faculty, and staff. Years later, and in the process of writing this book, I've thought a great deal about my professors' silence and the lack of direction they offered. To be blunt, you can't teach what you don't know. As I remember it, many of my nearly all White professors grew up in the upper and middle classes. They graduated from elite and highly selective colleges and universities, and those schools were the only types of institutions that they knew. Maybe I'm wrong, but I don't remember any instructors during my graduate studies who had worked in a higher education institution that wasn't at Harvard's level. As a result, they had little to teach me about securing employment and navigating a career in a public university; a small, nonselective liberal arts college; or even a historically black college or university (HBCU). In other words, schools that were, from their perspective, lower tiered and with less status were largely invisible and unknown.

Despite the absence of racially focused faculty mentors, my strongest, most powerful, and most enduring mentoring relationship was with Tracy Lynn Robinson. We were young when we were in graduate school, with much to learn about race and human behavior. We spent countless hours reflecting on our experiences as Black girls frequently forced into acts of resistance (although we didn't have the words then to describe what we were doing). We shared how we learned to push back when necessary and to stand up for our beliefs and identities as

Black women. In the beginning, we focused on racial identity and the character strengths passed on to Black daughters from their mothers. We discovered that resistance as a concept is deep and multifaceted and that not all resistance Black folks participate in serves us well in the long run. We collected and analyzed more data about resistance. We taught each other how to successfully write for scholarly publications, and we kept refining our ideas. Our partnership continued after graduate school. I conducted multigenerational research on Black teens and parents of Black teens, investigating messages they had received about race when growing up. Tracy eventually created multiple quantitative surveys to assess and measure optimal and suboptimal resistance. Most of all, we learned to return to the wealth of our cultural heritage, allowing the wisdom and strength of our sisters, mothers, and other mothers to guide our paths with open eyes and loving hearts.

In writing a book about mentoring Black female students, Tracy and I have necessarily returned to our younger selves. During my undergraduate years, I was the type of student who almost never reached out and asked for help. Although this strategy was somewhat unsuccessful, my personality and temperament led me to repeat these behaviors in graduate school. Representing myself as competent and always together was a life lesson taught to me by a mother who knew little of the professional White world her Black daughter was entering. So perhaps my professors never perceived me as wanting or needing their assistance. Such a performance was, I now realize, a resistance strategy I had developed—one that I thought would assure my survival in the elite educational institutions I had entered. But that adopted strategy was focused on my short-term needs, and over time, it made it harder for me to develop the tools that I might have used to admit my shortcomings and ask for help. Years later, I understand now that I truly needed a mentor.

Strong mentors consider what a mentee could or should be doing to advance her education and professional goals (whether the mentee has considered these possibilities or not). Mentoring across social differences asks that the mentor willingly share her social capital and that she do so with an awareness of the social position she occupies. This relationship has the potential to make visible the inner workings of class consciousness; mentors can exchange with their mentees the valuable knowledge derived from associations with those who have privilege and wealth. An effective mentor wouldn't leave the task of acquiring such information up to a mentee, especially not one who grew up with fewer economic resources and exposure to far fewer race- and class-based opportunities. In graduate school, I was fortunate to receive research experience with professors I deeply respected, along with recommendations and endorsements, publication opportunities, and public exposure of my work at a time when there were few other Black scholars studying Black girls. And for all that, I am enormously grateful. Yet as had been the case for me in the past, mentoring relationship gaps continue to persist for young Black women today. This book is written for college and university faculty who are willing to be *moral mentors*: individuals who will share their social capital by offering support, suggestions, and recommendations for professional advancement that are race and gender relevant, socially conscious, equitable, and fair.

Tracy's Mentoring Experiences

At a presentation on mentoring at the Women of Color in the Academy Conference, I spoke about the roles of good mentors, identifying that they were tutors, deliverers of constructive feedback, companions along the journey, wisdom sharers, role models, danger-up-ahead whisperers, cocreators of knowledge, stargazers, and speakers to the burning question of, "Do I stay or do I go?" Writing a book about mentoring Black college women has allowed me to reflect upon my relationships with mentors when I was a college student. What I have come to realize is that I never had a declared mentor.

Throughout college and graduate school, I have relied on other young people, and often on their parents, who stood in the gap of my motherless life. I lost my mother the day before I graduated from high school. I entered college less than three months later with a dilemma that occupied my thoughts: "What is life going to look like without my mother? And how am I going to manage?" Prior to my mother's death, my plan had been to stay in my hometown, attend college locally, continue working, and care for my ailing mother. As with any trauma, my life changed. On my eighteenth birthday, I applied to a college eight hours away from my home and, at the same time, applied for financial aid. My mother always taught me that I had to have an ace in the hole, and higher education was this ace. I felt her wind at my back as I had my gaze fixed on college.

In college, I was oblivious to the concept of mentors despite being in desperate need of a mentoring team. As a peer counselor during my junior year, I reported to a supervisor who was a graduate student. She listened actively and took interest in how I was doing in college in my role as a student leader. As peer counselors, each of us rotated the location of our monthly morning leadership meetings and were required to provide breakfast to the other student leaders in our individual apartments, which were subsidized by the college. I remember being convinced that I should be skipped; I was intimidated by the prospect of making breakfast for eight of my peers, two of whom were supervisors. My supervisor's insistence that I rise to the challenge was a watershed moment for me. I recall how she genuinely listened to my anxiety about cooking but offered no means of exit. Later, she raved over my scrambled eggs, which were not hard to make. After all, my mother had taught me how to make breakfast. The outcome was ultimately greater confidence and a sense of mastery. I learned to push past my preconceived notions of what I could and could not do.

Reflecting back on this memory, although I did not recognize it at the time, I had performance anxiety. I was on stage for all to see and felt scrutinized by my White peers as a Black girl at a Christian college that revered Whiteness, all in the name of Jesus. Race and racism were driving forces, but I lacked the skills to detect, name, and oppose this dynamic. I was the only Black person in that Peer Counselor Leadership group of eight, and one of a small handful of Black students on the entire campus. The silence surrounding the ubiquity of racism was profound. However, the position provided me with lodging and a stipend, critical for remaining in school and finishing my degree. The stakes were high.

The student development program at my undergraduate institution had close proximity to mentoring. As a peer counselor, I welcomed this opportunity for self-appraisal, outback wilderness experiences, leadership development, reflective prompts, and readings. I grew immensely, but my racial identity did not. The program was strangely silent about race, as was the entire curriculum. How did this silence happen during the 1970s era? After all, we were located in Southern California, just thirty-five miles east of Los Angeles, where scholarly writing, poetry, and artistry flourished. Black, Asian, Latino, and feminist power voices were rising. People were writing, speaking, protesting, performing, marching, singing songs, and sharing stories of resistance. The literature on racial, ethnic, and sexual identity development grew significantly during these years. Yet on my small Christian college campus, this energy, vitality, and scholarship was woefully missing. To identify and interrogate my proximity to the drape of Whiteness required a politically active community that did not exist.

During my senior year of college, I became even more attuned to how overt and loud racial silence was on campus. I recall asking the college president why there were no Black and Chicano faculty on campus. He stated that the only applications for employment from Blacks and Mexicans were for maintenance positions. Despite the racial silence, my experiences as a student leader fortified my sense of confidence. I doubt if I would have applied to graduate school without the leadership experiences, interpersonal relationships, and physiological safety that my college provided.

After leaving college, I started graduate school at Harvard. My Black academic peers furnished me with the substantial racial community that I was missing. Learning from them about race and how they successfully navigated racism in their academic and personal lives was akin to receiving a new pair of glasses. This new way of seeing the world allowed me to envision more clearly my place in it as a young Black woman.

I arrived at graduate school eager, excited, and exceptionally poor. It was a good day, and a rare one, when I had enough money to buy both a fifty-cent cup of coffee from Warburton's in Harvard Square and afford a fifty-cent token to ride the MBTA bus to my work-study job. More stressful than the academic work was the calculus of how to rub two pennies together. Along the way, there were kind souls—angels, I call them—who sensed my vulnerability and offered me advice on education, jobs, opportunities, even layering clothing for cold weather. My circle of school friends was vital to my comfort, retention, and success. There was no topic outside the scope of discussion.

Although none of us was rich, there were differences among us regarding financial and social capital. Some of us received formal mentoring from faculty, and some of us did not. The haphazard approach to mentoring students who are all in need of the commodity and benefits of mentoring means that inequity is inevitable. Lack of mentoring has far-reaching economic, occupational, emotional, and social consequences. My group of sisters and brothers were fabulous and generous, freely sharing their knowledge with me. But what would it have meant to be mentored by a faculty member who intentionally prepared me for the professoriate or for a research career? Given that I was not formally mentored, I questioned, albeit privately, why I had not been chosen and taken under the wing of a faculty member. I assumed that my lower-tiered Christian college, as well as not being part of an esteemed faculty member's prestigious research lab, marked me as less worthy of investment and not promising enough. The elitism of higher education is real and it cares an awful lot about students' pedigree, position, and prestige.

What must the mentee do and who must the mentee be to have a mentor offer their time, treasure, and talent to the growth of a yearning young adult? These private queries were my own. For me to have arrived at graduate school was a feat in and of itself, and though I saw the power, pride, and promise in my journey, I still wondered: What did the mentored students possess that I did not? I neither knew how to nor did I dare to initiate such bold conversation to answer my questions.

At their best, mentoring programs identify, train, and support mentors who in turn cultivate a meaningful relationship with their mentees. A bond exists in this shared space. Investment in the mentee's success is nested within a tradition of apprenticeship, sharing wisdom and craft over time because the mentor has a belief in the mentee's potential and commits to shaping the next generation.

Although I have never had an identified mentor, I had people who functioned as mentors, looking out for potholes and land mines that I had no awareness of. During my first year in the doctoral program, I needed TMJ surgery that would result in my jaw being wired shut for six weeks. Because of a congenital overbite, not to mention years of anxiety-related teeth grinding, surgery was required to realign my bite and to relieve chronic pain. After surgery, I needed to take nutrients through a straw. At the time, I lived in a dorm with a kitchen down the hall and shared a refrigerator with over twenty women on my floor. A better solution was needed. Janie Ward and her angel mother anticipated what I could not see and purchased a ton of green food, pureed it, and packed it in their freezer for me.

During the second year of my doctoral program, I was a graduate resident advisor. In this role I received housing and a stipend and did meaningful student development work. But my financial situation was still bleak. Having grown weary of my chronic whining about a lack of money, Janie told me, "Get a real job." Well! I did not appreciate her words, and yet they lit a fire under me. I applied for a Woodrow Wilson Fellowship, and this action introduced me to a career in counseling. For two years, I worked at a historically Black college in North Carolina as the director of counseling. In this environment, I blossomed professionally, personally, and academically. I was also able to collect data, free of charge, for my dissertation. After graduate school, my dissertation advisor helped me secure my postdoc, for which I was truly grateful.

Good mentors anticipate their mentees' developmentally appropriate indecision, confusion, and ambivalence while growing their mentees' competence and confidence. Had I known that intentional mentoring existed as a protected space for guidance, growth, and gentleness, I would have been bolder with risk-taking and mistake making. I would have been more compassionate about my naivete and recognized my vulnerability due to the concurrent stressors in my life.

My challenges were many, but my assets were greater. I had faith in God, a community of people who loved me, and the benefit of nearly eighteen years of exceptional mothering. My mother was the original Sister Resister, having taught me early that I would have to "run twice as fast to get half as far." Her words clarified my path. Her edict was to run long and hard, not to win the accolades of a discriminatory society but to embrace the goodness in life and to expect greatness from myself. My father never missed a graduation. He showered me with his wisdom and introduced me to colleagues who were caring and helpful. My grandparents, siblings, aunties, stepmother, uncle, and precious cousin poured sweetness into my life and anchored me through adulthood.

Janie has had an indelible impact on my scholarship, resistance, identity, decision-making, and sense of family that is divinely inspired. I like to think that our mothers are close girlfriends in heaven. We dedicate this book to all the young Black women who rely on skilled and competent mentors. Sister Resisters, across race, hue, ethnicity, and a host of differences, shine brightly your lamps to illuminate paths and commit to using your skills, truth, and conviction with your mentees. They need you in ways that they themselves can scarcely comprehend or voice.

Sister Resister Mentoring Model Overview

I N THIS BOOK, we explore the ways in which Black college women are currently underserved due to the challenges faced by mentors who do not yet possess the requisite skills to effectively guide Black women. When we refer to *mentors*, we mean faculty, administrators, academic staff, student development personnel, college instructors, advisors, mental health counselors, coaches, and trainers who are responsible for working with the young Black women on campus. When we speak of the work that mentors do, we are identifying much more than simply checking in with a student mentee to ask how her courses are going or offering to take her out to lunch for a chat. Across these pages, we present a very different model of mentoring Black female college students, one that centers the racialized and gendered social and political terrains that Black women are required to navigate. We argue that most mentors in higher education today seldom place this knowledge at the forefront of their mentoring work.

In these pages, we explore what can happen when attention is focused on understanding why, how, where, and when Black women must detect, name, oppose, and replace racial, gender, and social class bias in the college environment. This knowledge is key for preparing mentors to support their mentees' resistance to negative social pressures. We will demonstrate that being an effective mentor requires more than recognizing Black female mentees as individuals or as members of particular social groups. It calls for an examination and appreciation of how the mentor herself has been oriented to and shaped by her own racialized and gendered experiences. We argue that a mentor's readiness for intentional and deliberate engagement with Black female college students is dependent on these competencies.

There are several key features in this pioneering work. The first is the importance of *building mentoring relationships that are critical and intentional*. In this book, we argue that there is essential foundational knowledge that mentors must acquire in their work with Black female college students. A precise working knowledge of African American history is critical. It emphasizes social, political, and psychological resistance undertaken by Black people throughout the four hundred years of their presence in the United States, from enslavement to the present day. And this history promulgated colonialism worldwide.

Black Americans, as well as many other people of African descent now residing in the US, have been creating families, building communities, and living their lives under the drape of systemic racism—yet they have never been willing victims of the racial bias and discrimination inflicted upon them. When possible, we have exercised agency at the personal and collective levels. Today is no different. As we make explicit in the upcoming pages, Black women are facing a host of race-based challenges on college campuses, particularly in predominantly White institutions. The pressures and barriers they face are formidable and require unique culturally informed skills and dispositions for adept navigation. For this reason, we contrast our model of intentional mentoring with traditional mentoring models.

When it comes to ameliorating the effects of gendered racism, mentoring must be intentionally inclusive of Black college women's experiences as both Black and female. We reject the one-size-fits-all model of mentoring, as well as the idea that mentoring is primarily about creating relationships in which *the senior* is using their past personal or professional experiences to guide *the junior*. Instead, we articulate a mentoring stance that is critical, is reciprocal, and *at times will reflect a shift in the balance of power within the mentoring relationship*. Our model includes elements that are both instrumental and psychosocial. We maintain that there are situations in which Black women, including young Black women, know more about race, racism, and racial relations than do their White and often older adult mentors. According to sociologist Robin DiAngelo, White people suffer from "a lack of historical knowledge and an inability or unwillingness to trace the effects of history into the present."[1] Black people have racial knowledge that is historical and intergenerational. It is the knowledge of a people, perceived to be subdominant, who for the sake of their own liberation must know and understand the White dominant group far better than Whites know or understand the assumed subdominants.[2] At the same time, this knowledge held by Black people reveals an awareness that White people's presumed racial innocence is not an accurate representation of what is really going on. White Americans have used their skin color privilege to adopt a stance of racial innocence as a way of looking like they are positioned outside of the racial hierarchy—a hierarchy that they themselves created and continue to reinforce and count on.[3]

Black women and girls develop the tools to know, see, and name racism. A lack of awareness about racism can have a direct and deleterious impact on Black people; therefore we learn how to resist *not* knowing. Most importantly, Black parents, in socializing their children about racial realities, are acutely aware that an inability to teach their children about the ways, means, and motivations of those who uphold racial dominance (either wittingly or unwittingly) can inflict profound psychological and social damage.[4]

There are various levels of racism that Black women contend with: institutional or structural racism, personally mediated or interpersonal racism, internalized racism, environmental racism, and racism that involves White privilege.[5] Irrespective of the specific nature of racism, Black women's lived experiences with bias and discrimination equips them with expertise in this subject. This knowledge far outweighs the understanding of race that most White Americans bring to the table.[6]

Understanding gendered racism and knowing how it affects Black women in the college years allows a mentor to be purposeful in her work across social differences. Intentional mentoring requires a willingness to critically examine our cross-racial relational dynamics and interrogate our racial and gendered identities. We refer here to the identities of both the mentor and the mentee. Building self-awareness begins with consciousness-raising about racism, sexism, heteronormativity, and class elitism. In partnership, the mentor and her mentee can collaboratively develop a repertoire of culturally relevant attitudes, skills, and interventions. This book is designed to address these much needed relational and strategic elements.

Juxtaposed with the challenges faced by Black college-aged women, we place our analysis in an *ecological framework of life span developmental theory* that investigates multiple and concurrent changes in the individual that occur over time and across contexts. We identify developmental tasks and psychosocial competencies that demand the attention of women and girls of African descent in their late adolescent and young adult years. These women have unique needs that are informed by economic, psychological, biological, social, and historical realities that this text will discuss.

Another key element of our work is its focus on *the intersectionality of race with other dimensions of identity*.[7] Here we build on the theoretical formulations of Black feminism and womanism as both are culturally specific conceptualizations that integrate the legacy of Black women's experiences, theories, and knowledge production.[8] Girls and women of African descent are diverse. Our intersectional approach to this heterogenous group attends to much more than the fact of Black women's multiple identities. It acknowledges and avows that each of us exists within systems of oppression, domination, privilege, and discrimination. For example, Black transgender and gender nonconforming college students live at the intersections of racism, homophobia, and transphobia. While they are members of a demographic currently facing high levels of fatal violence, they are also innovative and brave survival strategists. Despite college campuses' acceptance of and openness to sexuality, marriage equality, and the encouragement of self-expression, gender nonconforming Black girls and women too often find that the landscape they must traverse is particularly treacherous across contexts and time.[9]

In these pages, we explore the tasks and competencies undertaken by Black college-aged women as outlined in life span developmental theory. We are applying a racially centered focus on intersectionality in Black women's lives. It is critical to understand how these women are positioned in relation to the psychological and social conditions that disadvantage many of them and privilege others. These disadvantages and privileges become most evident when we examine how young Black women confront chronic inequity circulating around and within their lives. As psychologist Stephen Vassalo writes, "Development is inseparable from culture, ideology, power, politics, and history. There is no such thing as a neutral and value free developmental idea, but rather, viewing students developmentally is a political, cultural, ideological, and historical act."[10]

Our book is motivated by what Michael Nakkula and Eric Toshalis call *reciprocal development*.[11] This notion, which is fundamentally relational, suggests that *dual and interactive developmental processes transpire in both the Black female student mentee and her mentor*. As we will show, mentors in predominantly White colleges and universities are most often White women as this demographic is overwhelmingly employed in student affairs, counseling, and other student support positions. By adopting the idea of reciprocal development, we will show how critical elements of Black students' identity and social development unfold alongside developmental elements that are simultaneously unfolding in the White mentor. In other words, in the mentoring relationships that we advocate, the White women mentors are growing emotionally and intellectually too. These recursive developmental moments interact, meaning both women will likely experience cognitive dissonance. It is also our hope that both the mentor and the mentee will inspire one another's growth. Such relational dynamics between Black and White women have implications for trust, team building, and program success and must be understood for their opportunities, histories, and barriers. We argue that this interactional space contributes to the co-construction of foundational knowledge needed to support positive psychosocial development and educational achievement in Black college women.

In addressing gendered racism and designing the effective strategies that assist women of African descent, our book argues that professional support staff working with Black women who wish to mentor competently will likely have self-assessment work to do themselves. Elsewhere, we have discussed the importance of resistance in the healthy psychological development of Black girls and women.[12] By focusing on the high-stakes developmental period of emerging adulthood, *we highlight the crucial role of resistance in the lives of women across race and ethnicity.*

When we refer to *resistance*, we are speaking of the conscious refusal to become stifled by race- and gender-based victimization or to accept an ideology of victim blame. We see resistance as an aspect of what scholars have identified as an asset-based cultural wealth of African Americans.[13] Resistance is a feminist and womanist epistemology.[14] What this means is that there is a high value placed on personal experience and the critical perspective of the world that one gleans from their social and political position. Such knowledge mitigates denying one's own needs in the service of others; it fosters self-esteem and it empowers Black resistance to disconnection and to racial oppression. But not all resistance is healthy and optimal; some methods of resistance are survival oriented: short-sighted and ill informed. As such, suboptimal resistance can be unhealthy and may exacerbate existing difficulties.[15]

When well-chosen and executed thoughtfully, *intentional mentoring practices should identify optimal resistance as a core competency to be nurtured and respected.* We have shown how African Americans can, in four steps, read, name, oppose, and replace racism. In our model, resistance is directly connected to optimism, agency, and resilience in Black women, particularly during early adulthood. This book examines why this is so and how educators, mentors, and others can work to access relational resources that support healthy resistance in Black women.

At the heart of this book is our belief that mentors in collaboration with Black women mentees can think through, design, and implement effective resistance approaches on college campuses. When doing so, mentors become *Sister Resisters.* As we describe in the upcoming chapters, becoming a Sister Resister is an ongoing process. We have found that many White women tend to mentor Black women initially from an unexamined sense of ubiquitous Whiteness, the point from which everybody else is and should be compared. This is due to two reasons: First, these mentors are working with an absence of meaningful information about their mentees—that is, Black cultural knowledge. Second, mentors are often unaware of the importance of exploring assumptions they themselves hold regarding their own gendered and racial realities.

In their role as mentors, as influencers of impressionable young Black women's decisions, direction, and development, White female mentors have essential self-work to do. Across race, women are socialized to privilege others' knowledge (e.g., White men), perceiving them to have more authority, relevance, and credibility about their lives than they themselves have. Patriarchy and body policing, chronic feelings of inadequacy, the drive to be perfect, the disease to please others and to always be nice, the chronic search for outside validation, saying yes when wanting to say no, and overfunctioning are critical issues that require White women's resistance.

Some scholars have explained that White women need "to think through race" and resist being silent in the presence of racism.[16] This means making visible previously unrecognized White norms of racial domination and privilege to expose the influence of racism on their lives. This work can be done through readings, attending workshops, webinars, and other sources of information. However, there is only so much that can be learned from a book or attendance at a conference. As a consequence of interrogating Whiteness, White women can gain a deeper understanding of their own and others' racial history, explore their personal and collective identities, and examine the relationships among Whiteness, patriarchy, racism, and power. To be clear, some White women have a history of exploring the relevance of race in their lives, often as a function of a stigmatized identity that they may embody (e.g., being of large size or having a physical disability or severe mental illness). This racial knowledge can be a tremendous asset to mentors in their work with Black women.

We call attention here to the extraordinary learning opportunity that is created for mentors when they are in active, ongoing engagement with their mentee. It is when these women are in relationship with one another that the opportunity for transformation begins. We have found that it is in the context of the mentoring relationship—that is, through interaction, dialoguing, and the sharing of stories together—that Black women are able to educate mentors about the racial inequities and disparities they are facing. Mentees can encourage White mentors to think about the need for resistance in White women's lives. As White female mentors realize the need to resist the systemic injustices that they themselves face, they may develop deeper respect for how their Black female mentees name and actively oppose gendered racism as it shows up on college campuses. White women, in their relationships with their mentees, can learn how to resist denying an essential truth—that the toxicity of chronic oppression is equally dangerous for White women too, including themselves. With this knowledge, White mentors recognize the value of resistance and can assemble a repertoire of resistance tools for their own empowerment. They can then use these tools in their work of co-constructing effective strategies with, for, and on behalf of their Black student mentees.

Writer and civil rights activist Maya Angelou wrote, "You may not control all the events that happen to you, but you can decide not to be reduced by them."[17] These words reside at the center of the resistance our work is built upon. We hope that together Black female students and their White mentors will work side by side to push back against those conditions that diminish women's lives while standing up for those values that uplift women during this critical time.

In this book, we focus on specific aspects of Black women's development that unfold in the college-age years. These include identity construction at the individual and group levels, intellectual development, appearance and demeanor, negotiating microaggressions and gendered racial stereotypes, and relational connections and disconnections. We realize there are many other areas that are being developed during these years of emerging adulthood and many additional barriers that readily derail young Black women. However, in this book we attend to those listed previously for the following reasons. First, we feel these are the areas that recur in the research literature, including in our own studies. Second, these are the issues that students bring to us privately in our offices, and they are the topics that faculty of color and their allies frequently discuss. And finally, we feel that these are the challenges that present opportunities for growth in young Black women mentees and the White mentors working with them. Let's consider the story of a faculty member named Barbara.

Mentoring Matters and Black Female College Students

Barbara has been on the faculty for five years. She feels good about her teaching and especially enjoys working with undergraduates in and outside of the classroom. But when the email invitation popped up on her computer announcing the start of a mentoring program on campus and seeking faculty mentor volunteers, a momentary look of anxiety crossed Barbara's face. She was pleased that the funding finally came through to support BIPOC, low-income, and first-generation students in the college and that recruitment for the program was set to begin. But a flurry of concerns kept Barbara from placing a sign-up call: Do I have the knowledge and experience to pass on to a group of students whose backgrounds are so very different from my own? I wonder if a Black woman would be more effective than I would be at mentoring a Black college woman?

We have written this book for Black college students and for the Barbaras in their lives. Faculty, administrators, and staff members who are finding themselves in work situations where they are being asked to step outside of their comfort zone and training to work with students whose backgrounds may differ from their own. Like Barbara, many college-based professionals who have been invited to mentor Black students face these nagging fears—of feeling inadequate for the challenge, of fearing mistakes, of saying the wrong thing (particularly about race), and of exposing the scope of their racial limitations to students.

Women, in particular, in feeling pressure from perfectionism, may labor under an assumption that there is only one right way to mentor Black students and may be scared to death that they will not master this elusive one right way of mentoring. Moreover, White women seldom have close friendships with Black women to whom they could turn for assistance. Due to the forces of White segregation—apathy and fragility—White women rely on racialized comfort, which supports silence and inaction against racial oppression.

Despite these fears, we are confident that there are White mentors in our midst who are ready and willing to step forward and commit to being Sister Resisters. College professionals who work through racial dissonance discover that this "is not a time of panic or disruption: it is a decision point—that moment when one reaches an intersection and must turn one way or the other."[18] Many future mentors are in that space, shaken to their moral core by the recent national attention to racial injustice and the historic maltreatment of people of color in this country. No longer willing to watch and wait for someone else to jump-start antiracism initiatives on campus, they are ready to direct their energies toward pushing back against the forces of racism and sexism negatively impacting the students they teach. The strategies we offer are designed to support mentors entering into this space as they build their capacity for meaningful cross-racial engagement.

Mentoring as Development in Action

The act of mentoring is the work of supporting the intellectual, emotional, and social development of college students in their early adulthood years and beyond. Growth can be activated by the experiences students are exposed to, most often with students in their age cohort. Development also can be activated by the interpersonal experiences that unfold between a mentor and a mentee. We believe that both the mentor and mentee are growing and changing over time, and their developmental trajectories interact in ways that can facilitate or impede maturation processes. Although we call for mentoring practices that build strong relationships of mutual respect, we realize that mentoring relationships may not always transpire so successfully. This book examines the interactional dynamics and discursive movements that emerge from the work undertaken within cross-racial connections. We also analyze the problematic interactions that are associated with relational disconnections as they play out in mentoring matters across social differences.

There are many different types and purposes of mentoring on college campuses. The most common type is one-to-one mentoring, and it is generally delivered by a volunteer mentor, like Barbara. These mentoring programs are either formally or loosely organized by faculty, administrators, or staff on campus. They might emerge from disciplinary departments or from extracurricular campus programming (e.g., culture-specific projects like a Black student organization or another ethnically based, religiously based, or other affinity group). Often, mentoring programs are targeted for specific populations who have been identified as needing extra assistance, like first-generation students. Programs might be specifically focused on career development to prepare for professional life after graduation. Role modeling, in which a mentor passes on knowledge, skills, and values that are deemed relevant to personal and ultimately professional success, is central to many mentoring initiatives. Some mentoring programs offer instrumental support in an effort to promote a mentee. In traditional mentoring programs, the role of the mentor is to be a sponsor. That "senior" level person presumably knows the ins and outs of an organization and uses that knowledge to help a junior mentee successfully enter and navigate her way through a college setting or through the stages of a professional career.[19]

Our mentoring model incorporates elements from traditional mentoring models, but we expect more from these relationships. When we use the term *mentoring* we are referring to those professional relationships that include instrumental, psychosocial, and political elements. We believe that mentoring should be informed by the critical theories that help the mentor understand their role in effectively addressing BIPOC students' socially constructed marginalization. In a world where Whiteness is overvalued, the impact of this oppression on mentees is profound.[20] In these pages, intentional mentoring integrates elements from our four step model—read it, name it, oppose it, and replace it—designed to help young Black people decode, discover, and discuss the inequalities they face.[21] With this knowledge, resistance strategies can be cultivated and put into action.

Anticipatory socialization—more specifically, antiracism awareness and training—promotes proactive agency, which in turn helps young Black women resist internalizing demeaning scripts steeped in gendered racism. A disastrous consequence of such scripts is that Black women view themselves as inferior and inadequate. We encourage Sister Resisters to embrace a moral stance whereby they create a caring space that is supportive and enables them to work through racial tensions that impede the mentoring relationship.[22]

The model we propose has the potential to foster a higher level of interpersonal honesty, trust, and intimacy—core elements of any authentic and healthy relationship. But talking about racism is difficult. Indeed, focusing on the negative impact of any of our marginalized social identities is difficult. Some mentors prefer to avoid such conversations. Too often we operate under an idealized, conflict-free image of mentoring, where needs are always met, conflict and discomfort are minimal, and the work of mentoring is mutually relevant, pleasing, and productive. But relationships that are chronically amicable, with unceasingly compliant mentees, often means that something important is being missed. Moreover, silence tends to have destructive consequences on a relational bond.

Racial conflict is a major reason that the continuing and unre-solved debate persists regarding which mentorship pairing is better: same race or cross-race. Some argue that mentors should be matched with someone who comes from, or at least deeply understands, the culture of the mentee. Presumably, a same race mentor has knowledge about what mentees bring to, and perhaps struggle with, in their col-lege setting. Such an awareness can strengthen the mentoring alliance and secure trusting relational attachments. Most important, in these dyads, individuals may be enabled to bring up and discuss uncomfort-able topics with a level of honesty that may elude cross-race pairings. David Thomas found that the most productive cross-race mentoring relationships were those in which both parties shared the same strategy for addressing racial differences.[23] For example, if a mentor advocates that her mentee pull back, remain silent, and stay nonconfrontational in the face of a microaggression, and the mentee, feeling angry and dis-respected, disagrees with this approach, one could accurately predict things might not go well.

On the other hand, there are a host of reasons why same-race men-toring pairings may not work. Race matching treats race as the only identity that the mentor needs to be mindful of. Intersectionality insists that in addition to race, we must honor our mentees' multiple identi-ties, which include sexuality, class, ability, and religion. These and other salient identities require us to question misguided notions that Black people are monoliths and that their needs are all the same.

In many colleges and universities, race matching may not be possi-ble. Often there are not enough faculty and staff of color to be matched with the mentees who need them. And to be perfectly honest, not all same-race dyads are culturally effortless, nor do they always result in the positive outcomes hoped for. A Black mentee may choose not to have a Black mentor. They may feel more comfortable with a White or non-Black mentor. The mentee may believe that White mentors have knowledge and experience that has greater relevance, value, and social power in the long run. For these and other reasons not articulated, some cross-racial matchings may not be ideal.

That said, whether they find themselves in same-race or cross-race dyads, the individuals within these mentoring relationships must be able to handle race-based tensions that are likely to emerge. In our experience, there are some mentors whose behavior is problematic, and as a result, their mentoring practice often runs adrift. These mentors are unable to grasp the significance of addressing racial differences and as a consequence minimize racial incidents that their Black mentees divulge. Such behavior ignores the impact of race on Black students' intellectual, social, and psychological development and reflects a gross misunderstanding of how structural racism undermines Black student success. The mentor's inability or unwillingness to do her personal antiracist work could contribute to resentment toward others who maintain that such work is necessary. It is hardly surprising that this group of mentors may find their mentoring practices to be less fulfilling, less productive, and less meaningful.

Developing Differently and Together Through Mentoring

In their transition from adolescence to young adulthood, we are accustomed to thinking about Black students' exploration of their racial identity during the college years. The search for identities that are self-defined, rather than merely accepting identities assigned to them by others, often becomes a central developmental task.[24] What we need to remember is that often the mentor's racial identity is developing as well and that this transformation is taking place within the context of her relationship with her Black mentee. For example, a mentor engaged in intellectual self-work may begin by reading one of the many books that examines racism and White supremacy. Doing so encourages her to think deeply. This might represent the first time that she is giving thought to herself as a racial being in relationship to other White people, as well as people of color. Or maybe the mentee introduces her mentor to Black feminist science fiction, which contributes to the mentor changing the way she incorporates diversity of thought in her classes. Both individuals are coming to understand what it means to be a Black woman and a White woman, individually and in relationship to one another.

Very often, the interactions between these two people reflect the different stages of racial identity and race consciousness acquired by each person.[25] For example, race might be hypersalient for the young adult mentee who is starting to see herself as a Black woman unfairly burdened by a host of unjust racial and gendered barriers. She may be confused, frustrated, and impatient. Her mentor, on the other hand, might be at an initial point in her racial consciousness and White identity development. The mentor may just be beginning to think in racial terms, just starting to recognize her own skin color privileges, and may be newly aware that racism and sexism create very different life circumstances for Black women to navigate. Those two women are developmentally incongruent in that their ability to think through racial matters begins from very different starting points. Both women are attempting to simultaneously manage the intellectual, social, and interpersonal challenges demanded of them while endeavoring to build a meaningful cross-racial mentoring relationship.

Despite the mismatch, powerful and growth-producing work can be undertaken within this mentoring relationship. We would even argue that mismatches are more likely the norm and not the exception. As an empathic, purposeful, and self-reflective "learner," the mentor can strengthen her knowledge about the impact of systemic oppression on her life and on her mentee's life. In other words, although these women may bring differences to the table, and their relationship may at first seem fraught and filled with pitfalls, the potential exists for growth in both women as they inspire development in each other.

In this book, we present case studies and narratives that explore the ways in which identity journeys interact between mentors and mentees. On college campuses, mentors can play an essential role in helping Black female mentees develop healthy and effective resistance and resilience strategies. We see this as the work of achieving core competencies needed to navigate the inequity they will face during and beyond the college years.

We know that very often mentors receive little or no training to become effective mentors, much less effective mentors with students of a different race. Some colleges assume that faculty and staff mentors already know all they need to know to be a good mentor, even if they are matched cross-race. Frequently, conversations and direct instruction about how to facilitate honest dialogue about race and racism is avoided. Indeed, explicit discussion of racial matters frequently gets sidestepped or is made comfortable by overintellectualizing to the point of being irrelevant. Cross-racial relationships that do not openly address sociopolitical matters are inauthentic and lack accountability. Self-examination must be paired with personal and collective action. It is within intentional mentoring relationships that mentors and mentees can undertake the real work of campus inclusion and challenge policies and practices that fail to uphold the ideals of equality and social justice in higher education.

In this book, we illustrate how mentors can do more than demystify the cultural norms and expectations of college life. We expect them to do more than clarify for mentees what it takes to be successful in college and in their future professional lives. We maintain that mentors working across racial differences must be brave enough to challenge the status quo and accept the conflict that will most likely ensue. That could mean speaking up and pushing back against institutional elements that uphold sexism, racism, heterosexism, and classism. This may mean that cherished values and campus cultures that produce and normalize racial inequalities are called out as unfair. Mentoring with and advocating on behalf of Black female students demands that the personal become political. For this reason, ignoring race talk will not do. Nor will it work to demand that any talk about racism or other racial topics be calm and rational. Tamping down the affect involved in race talk may make White mentors feel better, but such demands are patently unfair to mentees of color. Pushing back against the negative effects of injustice on campus is hard work and young Black women need allies to help them develop key tools, requisite attitudes, and skills so they can resist—and stay resilient.

In the college years, Sister Resisters can perform that role. More mentors are needed who understand resistance in combating identity threats and psychological assaults. This book offers readers an examination of the importance of resistance for women of African descent historically and illustrates why resistance continues to be needed today. With the development of thoughtfully designed, culturally based skills, we offer ways in which mentors, particularly White female mentors, can become confident in the essential role they play in their mentee's life. In addition, we trust that mentors will become proficient in co-constructing with Black women the effective methods of resistance and appropriate plans of action.

On college campuses, Native, Arab, Latina, and Asian women often contend with issues that are similar to those faced by Black women. Although our focus is on young Black college women, much of what we are saying is applicable to other student populations. May *Sister Resisters* take to heart the mentoring model on these pages and share this knowledge to uplift and empower all the women that we mentor.

CHAPTER 1

Understanding Black Women on Predominantly White Campuses

THEORY AND APPLICATION

"If there is no struggle, there is no progress."

—Frederick Douglass

THE EXISTING RESEARCH LITERATURE regarding Black women's gendered and racial experiences in higher education is considerable. Yet the people who are called upon to function as mentors are often unaware of this research and thus know little of the circumstances surrounding Black college women's lives. What they need to know is the wide range of institutional factors that function as roadblocks to the well-being of Black college women, particularly in predominantly White institutions. Note here that we highlight the underlying forces of racism because of its deeply pernicious roots, present in the founding of nearly every institution in our nation. It is not our intention to diminish the impact of other oppressions, but we argue that sexism, class elitism, and ableism are made worse when they align with the enduring legacy of racial discrimination.

Campus Climate

Researchers offer clear evidence that campus cultures at predominantly White institutions often contribute to Black students and other students of color feeling discounted and unwelcome. Black women lament that the students who look like them are perceived as undifferentiated and interchangeable. Black female students say they are stared at in objectifying ways and complain of being exposed to racially insensitive comments at the library, in study halls, and in other spaces on campus.[1] Other students report more subtle signs of prejudice, such as being regarded with suspicion or being presumed incompetent, criminally prone, and affirmative action admits.[2]

"One time," explained Leila, a junior in the art department, "because these people can't see the differences between us, my friend was singled out by campus security after an incident at a dorm party that got a little loud. As far as those security guards were concerned, Black people, meaning all of us Black people, are criminals, criminal wannabees, or criminal gonna-bees!"[3]

Leila's story describes the prevalence of campus-based animosities and microaggressions in Black student life. Although universities aspire to be inclusive and welcoming of ethnic and racial diversity on campus, research highlights the pervasiveness of microaggressions for Black female students, staff, and faculty alike.[4] Defined as brief and commonplace indignities expressed through verbal or behavioral means, *microaggressions* communicate hostile, derogatory slights and insults to targeted, usually minority, social groups.[5] Students who experience racial microaggressions begin to feel alienated in spaces where these oppressions occur.[6] Black women are particularly impacted by the relational injuries caused by microaggressions. For some, microaggressions feel worse than blatant racism as the perpetrators are often living in one's dorm or are classmates or share one's program of study. Black students told us that often these subtle cruelties are not from unknown or anonymous people who happen to attend their college; they are expressed by students who Black students had thought were their friends.[7]

Interracial tension within the residence halls creates uncomfortable living conditions for students of color. They are othered in their dorm rooms, where their hair and grooming practices exist as a source of endless fascination: "How do you wash your hair? Why do you put oil in it? What happens when it rains?" Fitting in and feeling comfortable in a new environment can be difficult when a Black woman is seen as different, unknown, and unknowable. The relational wounds inflicted in these noninclusive campus climates make it hard for Black college women to feel that they belong. Feeling excluded can interrupt academic success. In addition, toxic living environments decrease the likelihood that Black women will sustain relationships across social differences with students, their faculty, and staff.[8]

Staff and faculty who work regularly with Black college women have seen their momentum disrupted when they feel that they do not matter and that their concerns are dismissed.[9] Heightened feelings of loneliness and invalidation produce anxiety. The resulting depression often contributes to, or at times exacerbates, preexisting mental health issues already present in Black women's lives.[10] Classroom experiences can feel unwelcoming as well. Black students report that professors treat Black students as indistinguishable from one another, often calling them by the wrong name and mispronouncing uncommon names. In many predominantly White institutions, not only are faculty of color in small numbers, Black students also find themselves one of a handful in their classes, with few peers to study and interact with from their own backgrounds. In many academic disciplines, course curriculum continues to display cultural biases as students of color see a lack of representation in the topics and materials they are expected to master. Black students report feeling intellectually belittled in class, their contributions often ignored or repackaged as someone else's ideas, for which they do not receive credit. Often chosen last for course-required group projects, Black students are expected to be spokespeople for the entire race, or their solicited racialized experiences are devalued all together. Most troublesome, many students complain that they feel burdened to educate their White college peers and professors about being "the minority" while simultaneously feeling pressured to conform to the majority when engaging in academic pursuits.[11]

Most students, even the strongest and most successful, might require a little help now and then, so colleges and universities make academic and allied support services available on campus. But all too often, in financial aid, career services, and academic support offices, Black female students complain that they do not receive the support they need. Services and programs are generally designed for a generalist student population, most often read as White and middle class. As a result, some university support staff hold insufficient understandings of Black students' concerns. The academic pressures, financial burdens, overlapping and often conflicting social responsibilities, and career concerns among students of color are often not seen.[12] Despite our assertions of being "student centered," institutions of higher education are remiss in designing academic advising, mental health counseling, financial aid, disabilities services, residence life, and health and wellness services with nontraditional students in mind.

Emily represents a student whose interactions on campus as Black and hearing-impaired provide a compelling illustration of how ableist thinking complicates her ability to secure an education. An academically strong and diligent student, Emily is confused and frustrated after an unpleasant interaction with a professor in her department. The course instructor had refused her extended time on an assignment, arguing that since she had such a high GPA, her disability must not be all that disabling. Emily struggled to explain herself, but the professor appeared annoyed with having to listen to the cadence of her speech and seemed generally uninterested in what she had to say. Later, speaking with the other students in the only deaf student support group on campus, she discussed her dilemma. She shared her suspicion that because she is Black, the professor thought she was trying to cheat her way through her academic program by asking for extra time. Her deaf friends, all White, downplayed Emily's concerns about racial discrimination. They insisted that deafness and accessibility, not race, were the issues, and they vigorously asserted that she had a strong case to bring up with the disability services office. Now feeling doubly misunderstood, Emily wearily left the group. She was offended that her professor thought her to be dishonest and she felt invalidated by her deaf White friends who had only seen her as deaf, and thus minimized her identity as a Black woman.

While providing a much-needed service to students, groups on campus may think their advocacy is inclusive and intersectional, but that is not always the case. Advocating for the empowerment of one identity element (being hearing impaired) may inadvertently disempower other aspects of an individual's sense of self. Moreover, the sad truth is that too often personnel in student affairs offices are insufficiently trained in gendered racial sensitivity. Staff, too, may have missed Emily's vulnerability to being regarded as undeserving of her education, an accusation commonly charged against Black students (think of myths about affirmative action, diversity quotas, and racial preferences). As a hearing-impaired student, Emily knew how hard she had worked for her academic success and felt she deserved the few accommodational services the college provided—and which are mandated by federal law. Federal provisions are not enough to counteract the underlying suspicions college personnel may hold against Black students, nor do they eliminate the negating discourses associated with race, gender, and disability that too often presume students' inferiority.

Identity Work

I (Janie) was introduced to the poet Audre Lorde in graduate school. A classmate lovingly gifted me several of her books for my birthday. I walked around with crumpled, dog-eared copies of her short books of essays and poetry, the pages worn out from being over-read. Lorde wrote, "When I say I am a Black feminist, I mean I recognize that my power as well as my primary oppressions come as a result of my Blackness as well as my womanness, and therefore my struggles on both of these fronts are inseparable."[13] Black feminists first introduced me to the idea of oppression being situated at the intersection between race and gender. Later Black scholars went on to expand this idea. Audre Lorde, bell hooks, June Jordan, Kimberlé Crenshaw, and others forcefully argued that Black women occupy a special vantage point for our marginality that has given us a unique perspective to criticize racist, classist, and sexist ideologies and power dynamics. Most importantly, such oppressions have also taught us how to create counternarratives that oppose those whose interests lie in limiting how we see ourselves and others.

Young adulthood is a critical period in the development of Black college women as they transition from adolescence. Black women are a very diverse group of women with significant differences in social class, ethnic background, language, national origin, sexuality, geographic location, disability, and religion. For example, a Black college student could be a Somali Muslim working-class woman or a wealthy Pentecostal Trinidadian. Black women face multiple jeopardies and are forced to develop "multiple consciousnesses" due to the fact that inequality works both with and through intersecting sources of discrimination.[14]

Identity is a developmental construct based on the idea that as individuals mature, so too does their understanding of the self and the world. Black women bring to campus a wide range of prior knowledge about what it means to be Black individually and how they make sense of their group membership.[15] Western psychology reifies individuation and autonomy as the epitome of growth and development. But many African American psychologists argue that for Black individuals, positive identity is "an extended sense of self embedded within the African American collective."[16] This extended sense of self serves as a protective factor related to identity development.[17] On college campuses, race and ethnicity are often treated as synonyms. The descriptors are lumped together and assumed indistinguishable, yet the reality is that they differ considerably. Black ethnic groups living in the United States hail from different parts of the African Diaspora (e.g., Senegalese, Caribbean, Afro-Brazilian). Their ethnic identity might be based on ethnic or national pride, immigration status, or acculturation, as well as interracial and intraracial relationships. Depending on their background, students may come to campus having been raised in families that seldom talked about race or in families that prioritize mainstream middle-class values and ethnic culture above race. There are families of African descent who feel racism has diminished to the point that it is less important to emphasize protective strategies in their childrearing practices. For these reasons, the developmental work of integrating a positive sense of self with an identity that includes being a member of a devalued group may differ significantly within our school's Black student population.

Black students in college are exposed to an array of conversations that may lead them to think about racial identity differently than before. For Black women, college can become a transformative moment where some students confront their pro-White preferences or interrogate their own internalization of anti-Black attitudes for the very first time. In and outside of classrooms, Black women are introduced to new ideas that cause them to question, explore, and place greater (or lesser) value on the meaning of being Black. Many Black college women immerse themselves in the process of reimagining what it means to be a member of a social group whose history includes unrelenting racial oppression and incredible survival alongside achievement against the odds. Racial pride and building strong connections to other Black people as their primary reference group can strengthen an ethic of care toward the larger Black community.[18] In their move toward internalizing a more secure racial identity, Black students may reflect more deeply upon their feelings about how race interacts with the many other social identities they possess. This is also when we may see or hear Black women express anger and resentment toward the racism and sexism they encounter as they work through the meanings associated with privilege and inequity.

As young Black women strengthen their racial identity development, redefining a sense of womanhood is critical to their resistance against the patriarchal values that beset women across race and ethnicity. Integrating one's gender and ethnic identities requires negotiation of the many social forces that can negatively define self-worth.[19] On college campuses, Black women struggle to find spaces where their identities can be affirmed and celebrated. Like their White female counterparts, young Black women find themselves negotiating issues associated with being a woman in this society. For Black women, these issues include navigating perceptions of body image, weight and body shape, light skin color bias, the politics of their hairstyles, and the objectification of the female body.

Being a Black woman has always called for a heightened level of social and psychological resilience. Moving through barriers and challenging the status quo are required competencies given the chronicity of racial and gender-based discrimination in society. Many of our students are the first and often the only ones in their families to obtain a college degree, often while having the responsibility of taking care of others (children, siblings, adults). Once they finish their degrees, Black women will find that there are still many professional fields in which they will be the first or the only ones in their workplaces who look like them. Establishing community through connections with other Black students, especially Black women who are facing the same challenges, can serve as a protective factor for people of African descent. It is in these relationships that Black women feel their voices and experiences are accepted and their racial identities are validated.

A major undertaking for Black adolescent and college-aged women is to resist internalizing other people's definitions of who they are. When Black women fail to create an identity that is self-defined, they may succumb to stereotypic beliefs about Black women and doubt who they are and what they can do—constituting a crisis of identity and a disconnection from the self.[20]

Racialized and gendered stereotypes assigned to Black women's identity categories are alive and well on college campuses. Black women are unfairly labeled as uneducated, hypersexual, incompetent, and undeserving of their place in higher education. The Black superwoman is another powerful and dangerous stereotype that has become so entrenched that for some Black women, it is a cultural ideal.[21] The superwoman stereotype pressures Black women to portray themselves as superstrong and self-sacrificing.[22] These are psychological coping characteristics that presumably allow them to successfully overcome race- and gender-based stress and discrimination in their daily lives. Woods-Griscombe characterizes the superwoman role as an obligation to manifest strength by suppressing emotions. Superwomen resist being vulnerable or dependent. They feel obligated to help others and they are determined to succeed despite limited psychological and financial resources. Unfortunately, such portrayals of strength, which we have seen displayed on the campuses where we teach, may actually conceal serious anxieties and troublesome fears that are often unacknowledged or unknown, even to the Black student herself.

Along with the pressure to become superwomen, Black students also find themselves pushing against the "angry Black woman" stereotype. This is another socially ascribed "controlling image" that is intricately connected to gendered racism.[23] And the angry woman trope is unrelenting and terribly hard to shake off.

Sheila is a second-year history major. She moved to her campus on the East Coast from a Midwestern state, where she described her upbringing as "simple, boring, and pretty mainstream." Sheila thinks of herself as an even-tempered Black woman, never quick to anger and certainly not disrespectful when, on occasion, a situation does manage to tick her off. But lately she has felt like her classmates see her quite differently than she sees herself. It began, she explained, in class, when a discussion became heated and she found her voice volume increasing as she struggled to make her opinion understood. The discussion went back and forth, and although Sheila was alone in her opinion and had to argue tenaciously for her perspective, she left the class feeling pretty good about the interaction. Yet later on the stairwell, she heard several students from her class talking about the exchange, referring to Sheila as one of those "aggressive" Black women "with a chip on her shoulder."

The Black feminist scholar Patricia Hill Collins argues that far too many people outside of the Black community perceive anger as deeply engrained in the self-concept of Black women.[24] Denouncing that anger and labeling it as evidence of a character flaw is yet another way of controlling Black women's behavior. Presumed to be angry, bitter, and relentlessly resentful, Sheila and her peers may have to work over-time doing "impression management." They hold back and censor their voices, remaining silent and invisible rather than risking being seen on campus as difficult, mean, and unreasonable.[25] For a number of reasons, this strategy does not bode well for Black students. They fail to fully par-ticipate in the learning process. On a personal level, suppressing their emotions can be fatiguing and stressful. Not being open with others renders more difficult the forging of authentic connections. Finally, if Black women do not effectively learn to resist self-silencing as a strategy, they will not learn how to express dissenting positions in ways that allow their voices to be heard and their perspectives to be taken seriously.

At the heart of this work is our own theoretical construct of resis-tance. Throughout these chapters, we offer clearly illustrated examples of resistance strategies undertaken by Black women as an environmen-tal response to navigating the life challenges that come to the fore in the college context. We provide concrete recommendations for men-tors working with Black women that will nurture optimal strategies and identify and replace problematic suboptimal resistance strategies as they emerge among Black female student populations in the college years.

Resistance in Black Women's Lives

Resistance and resilience are essential skills that promote the healthy developmental outcomes that enable young Black women to interact effectively within their environments. Developing one's emerging gender and racial identity is a complex yet essential task in and of itself. This work is made all the more difficult when simultaneously resisting racialized gender bias, especially at predominantly White institutions.

For Black young adult women, a strong *critical consciousness*—"the ability to understand the oppressive social forces shaping one's community as well as the feelings of agency and commitment to challenging these forces"—is fundamental.[26] It enhances her ability to acquire and effectively apply the knowledge, attitudes, and skills to navigate through interpersonal and systemic racism and sexism. Critical consciousness has been found to impact social and economic outcomes, improve students' academic achievement, and help women manage emotions that emerge from confronting bias.[27]

Resistance Theory

In today's economic and global society, college attendance and graduation are essential to success and the acquisition of new technologies. In the traditional pathway to college completion, career and vocation-driven goals are coupled with a need to balance social and academic demands. Here too Black students encounter barriers obstructing their paths for future success. Many young adult Black women struggle to effectively respond to the challenges before them. Navigating these barriers to success is demanding. The work is emotionally and intellectually taxing, and it can deplete psychological reserves.

People of African descent have a long legacy of standing up, fighting back, speaking out, and asserting our moral authority in the face of continuing injustice, intolerance, and ignorance.[28] We know this task has never been easy, nor can we approach the task in ways that are careless, faint-hearted, or indecisive. Carefully designed approaches to resistance are necessary, and they require that the resister regulate her emotions under stress and think clearly about her next move. Adopting such an approach with Black college women is foundational resistance work. So too are elements that develop with heightened self-examination (e.g., knowing one's personal strengths and limitations, possessing self-confidence, having a strong moral character, and feeling connected to others through a sense of racial pride). In addition, resistance calls for another level of introspection from Black college women that includes the development of a critical consciousness to analyze social and political contexts. The importance of critical analysis serves double duty: with it, students can develop what we call a *liberatory consciousness*—one that releases her from the constraints of controlling stereotypes, low expectations, and low self-esteem. Resisting with a liberatory consciousness does not entail settling for a quick and immediate resolution to a problem. Doing so may work well in the short term, but it is usually at the expense of the thoughtful decision-making that considers long-term consequences. Second, when it comes to making decisions about next steps, Black women must appreciate the constraints they are operating under while taking calculated risks to meet their goals.

Black college students must develop the ability to read, name, oppose, and replace the bias and discrimination that they and other women of color face on campus.[29] This knowledge, along with the attitudes and skills outlined in this book, will help Black women to build a repertoire of strategies they can employ to understand and respond effectively to these negative forces.

It is important to be clear about what we mean by *resistance*. The term generally describes negativity, such as when a recalcitrant student refuses to obey her teacher. But when we use the term, we describe resistance as having four key elements: (1) It is functional, in that it serves as a means of pursuing an aim, or it is used to pursue an end goal. Resistance has a goal--personal and collective liberation. (2) Resistance strategies that Black women adopt can be positive or negative. (3) The resistance we highlight is about pushing back against the negating forces of oppression and taking a stand in support of a positive, self-affirming end goal. Finally, (4) there is a dialectical relationship between resistance and resilience, such that Black women who optimally resist in their social environment strengthen their ability to remain resilient.

To identify and name the strategies that could help Black women push against intersecting forms of social oppression, we developed a resistance theory for Black adolescent girls and women.[30] Its primary goal is to explain what Black women need to thrive in the face of racism, sexism, gender oppression, xenophobia, ableism, heteronomativity, and classism, and to help them acquire the skills that allow them to recognize and name those negative forces and oppose them in healthy ways.

The aim of healthy or optimal resistance is to aid Black women in replacing their reactions to perceptions of racism with responses that are affirming while managing their behavior in support of long-term healing. A primary benefit of healthy resistance is that it highlights the sociopolitical context of race in America and the role that inequity plays in shaping societal attitudes, beliefs, values, and behaviors. It can include *taking a stand* for those things that promote positive self-validation and group affirmation. Resistance also entails the ability to *withstand* negative social influences and to seek solutions that empower people through both a positive sense of self and the strengthening of connections to the broader Black community.

In contrast to optimal resistance, *suboptimal resistance* refers to short-term cognitive and behavioral adaptations to chronic stress that fail to provide tools that transfer to future crises in effective ways. They are self-destructive, which means they impair people psychologically by diminishing self-esteem, undermining self-efficacy, and distorting a sense of self that can lead people to behave in ways that cause injury to themselves and may create negative reactions in others. For example, suboptimal resistance can lead young Black women to internalizing a devalued racial status; succumbing to self-doubt, pessimism, lack of faith, or lack of pride; and refusing to seek support or guidance from strong and positive adult women. More specifically, suboptimal resistance fails to provide women with real control over damaging and dangerous situations. A consequence is that women are left stymied in their ability to make the changes that could bring them the respect and value they seek.

Although suboptimal resistance strategies do not serve Black women well in the long run and are self-alienating, nearsighted, and survival-oriented, they induce pleasure immediately and are soothing, even addictive. We see this on our college campuses when Black female students engage in substance abuse, comfort eating, self-loathing, selflessness, unprotected sex, and racial isolation from communities of support.[31] When Black women are locked in these suboptimal and unhealthy forms of resistance they often focus on the immediate (e.g., What can I do to make me feel better right now?) rather than on the larger picture (e.g., What can I do to make changes in my life that will improve my future social, academic, and interpersonal success?).

Table 1-1 compares resistance across the domains of feeling, doing, and thinking.

Black female college students must develop resistance strategies that are intentional and embody an oppositional gaze informed by their culture and political perspectives. This resistance fuses knowledge gained from personal reflection with a historical analysis and a deep understanding of the present-day conditions confronting Black people in America and throughout the world. It comes from being responsive to the knowledge that has sustained Black people across geographic spaces and throughout time. Cultivated in each of our subsequent generations has been the clarion call that *a belief in self must be far greater than*

TABLE 1.1   Sister Resister suboptimal and optimal affect, action, and awareness

Suboptimal affect	Optimal affect
Chronic feelings of victimization, inadequacy, inferiority, insecurity, and fear associated with historical and ongoing racism. Inability to regulate emotional distress.	Feelings of respect for Black people's survival. Optimism for Black people's resilience. Holding hope for the future and compassion for humanity's struggle against multiple oppressions.
Suboptimal action	**Optimal action**
Disordered reliance on substances, alcohol, food, gambling, sex, and external validation. Secrecy, deceit, and racial isolation. Impulsivity. Uncritically embracing the dominance of US culture.	Resisting the lie of perfectionism; striving for excellence. Setting boundaries; expecting justice. Asking for what you deserve. Pursuing dreams. Naming oppression. Delaying gratification. Asking for and receiving help.
Suboptimal awareness	**Optimal awareness**
Thinking that conditions will never change, that White people, culture, bodies, or histories are superior, that women are subordinate to men, or that able bodies are superior and more desirable.	Belief in the benevolence of the universe, that life is purposeful and that the world is better because we are alive. A belief in community empowerment and that together, people can change the world for good.

anyone's disbelief. This resistance is born from love, racial pride, relational strength, and purpose, not from hate, desperation, and brokenness.

As a developmental task, resistance takes root in adolescence and gains greater importance over time. Adulthood responsibilities require a thoughtful examination of who you are and what you wish your future life will be. For Black women, optimal resistance cannot exist without an established sense of identity (knowing who I am and where I belong), as well as a sense of communion with others. Learning how to interpret and honor one's dreams, knowing how to remember to trust one's voice and reclaim self-worth, even when it means swimming against the prevailing current of thought—these are the beliefs and behaviors of optimal resistance. Social positions may have evolved over time, but injustice and stratification continue to be deeply embedded throughout US culture. Despite the hostile environments inside and outside the doors of our college communities, we can create the contexts that young Black women need to nurture their characters, social connections, and academic competencies in order to allow them to thrive in school and beyond.

As the presence of Black women in higher education increases, there is a greater need for educators and allied personnel to better understand and strengthen their abilities to work with this increasing student population. Mentoring speaks to a host of activities that are thought to build strong and meaningful connections between college instructors and professional support staff working with Black female students on campus. When it is done well, these relationships foster psychological growth and promote students' intellectual, academic, and social development as they progress through college. This book is dedicated to the mentors who enter into such vitally important relationships with Black female college students. May we all grow together in allyship and love.

CHAPTER 2

Framing Resistance for Women

AT A WOMEN'S RIGHTS CONVENTION in 1851, the formerly enslaved abolitionist Sojourner Truth stood before a crowd of primarily White women. Drawing on her own personal experiences with racial and gender violence and political disenfranchisement, Truth argued forcefully that White women should expand their definition of womanhood and extend to Black women the same rights as those afforded to Whites.[1] Since then, standing in the shadow of Truth, generations of Black women have continued to call for a response to gender oppression that actively resists racism and sexism while honoring the humanity of women everywhere. In the following pages, we are extending an invitation to all women to examine the terms of their oppression. The starting point for each individual woman and the unique path she will pursue in her journey of self-discovery will necessarily differ. However, in the words of Audre Lorde, "the strength of women lies in recognizing differences between us as creative, and in standing in those distortions which we inherited without blame, but now are ours to alter."[2]

Resistance is critical to Black women's well-being, and in the previous chapter we focused on what resistance looks like for Black women. In this chapter, we present our theory of resistance to explore its relevance for White women. We illuminate the benefits that accrue when mentors integrate attitudes and behaviors of resistance into their lives and their mentoring practice. The mentoring relationship is a perfect setting to incorporate this work as the relationship is enriched when mentors and mentees engage in this interrogative process.[3] Resistance is needed for both groups of women as they build and sustain intentional and productive relationships across race. To do so requires understanding similarities and differences in each other's paths to resistance.

There are multiple realities we hold concurrently. We trust that women can bridge social identity differences by being willing to confront and resist the systems of power that contribute to adversarial relationships. As interlocking ideologies with reinforcing forms of power, patriarchy and Whiteness are intimate partners. This chapter discusses how White racial normativity (Whiteness), patriarchy, and White supremacist values and beliefs exert their authority on Black and White women, separately and together.[4] We do this to explore the dynamics that can interfere with communication between White women mentors and Black female students. These forces monitor and restrict women's lives, but we argue that such forces need not negate women's power to push back. Resistance is a means for women across race and ethnicity to acknowledge, honor, and respect the power that is theirs.

The theory of intersectionality calls for us to affirm that White women also embody complex identities, including "a privileged racial status, a subordinate gender status, and additional intersecting identities."[5] As is the case with Black women, the socially constructed meanings about these identities for White women do not act independently. They interact and contribute to various forms of inequality for them as well.

When we take into account the historical and political contexts that define gender, several factors become clear. Social scientists state that we live in a culture that upholds a set of overarching beliefs and ideas enforcing notions of sexuality and gender that equate to male supremacy, female inferiority, the primacy of heterosexuality, and the natural superiority of light skin human "races" over other "racial" groups. Patriarchy is intertwined with the elevation of Whiteness. Both are propped up by systems of power and cultural norms, and both are supported by tradition, education, mainstream religion, and rampant consumer culture.[6]

Race in the United States structures the lives of all people, irrespective of their skin color. Although racial experiences differ for Black and White women, all women inhabit and therefore must negotiate an array of social identities that exist within systems of oppression and privilege.

Across race, over time, and within different cultural contexts, women move in and out of positions of vulnerability and opportunity.

Understanding where and when we are vulnerable and when and where it is necessary to push back against oppression is essential to effective resistance. When discussing women and resistance, we reject a false binary that casts White women as unduly privileged across all domains of life and positions Black women as serially disadvantaged. At the same time, we do not wish to make a false equivalency here. White women's resistance is not the same as Black women's resistance. All women struggle under White supremacy and patriarchy, but certainly not in the same way. Racism and patriarchy are interrelated and mutually supporting systems of domination. Racism frames the experience of sexism differently for Black women and White women. Understanding this reality is critical to understanding the subordination of all women. In addition, we do not assume a uniformity of oppression. To do so would imply that all White women would implicitly know exactly what all Black women contend with, in every form of oppression that they face. Such thinking is not only blatantly wrong; it also obfuscates the need for White women to listen to and learn from Black women's voices.[7]

That said, we realize that, as of yet, Black and White women are hardly united in solidarity against the common battles that we face. For Black women, across class, ethnicity, sexuality, and age, both racial and gender oppression converge as gendered racism. White women are victimized by sexism too, but their racial capital offers them protections that Black women will never enjoy. However, those race-based benefits come with a cost. The patriarchal bind that confers race and gendered advantages to White women also renders them captive to a system that both demands and rewards their silence and obedience. For this, they pay a price. Women's voices may not be heard or taken seriously when they do speak up. For some, it may be easier to acquiesce to racism and sexism than to challenge these powerful oppressions. On the other hand, thankfully, as long as patriarchy has existed, some White women have resisted. It is within this tradition that this book resides.

To establish caring and intentional relationships between White women mentors and young Black women mentees, we encourage mentors to learn about the dynamics at play in Black women's racial and gender socialization. It is equally important for White mentors to also have insight into their own orientation regarding these constructs. Both groups of women are influenced, albeit in different ways, by the global centrality of Whiteness and masculinity. Ultimately, our goal here is to encourage White women to recognize their shared opposition to both different and overlapping oppressive forces.[8] We remind the reader that "racism is patriarchal. Patriarchy is racist (and) we will not destroy one institution without destroying the other."[9]

When done well, mentoring is an intensely relational activity. The women involved must be willing to establish a connection that facilitates trust between themselves and their mentees despite differences in race/ethnicity, age, most likely socioeconomic background, and other social factors. Trust is impeded when mentors and mentees struggle to appreciate the contributions and the challenges that each woman brings to the table. For example, sometimes insufficient attention is devoted to the relational knowledge and skills that Black students possess. Likewise, there are times when White mentors fail to appreciate that they need assistance in making cross-racial connections psychologically safe. One thing that hasn't changed is that Black female college students look to their White mentors for guidance, support, and wisdom. Very often, such guidance demands that both women feel a degree of comfort to ask questions and share their feelings, fears, thoughts, and concerns with each other.

How Whiteness Is Normalized

Building productive cross-racial relationships calls for us to take into account the ways in which women have been exposed to and socialized within toxic institutional structures. Fundamental to whiteness ideology is a belief in the hierarchy of skin color differences. The assertion of natural superiority granted to "lighter skinned" or White people over all other groups lays the groundwork upon which White normativity is built. Social scientists argue that Whiteness is "a socially constructed and maintained ideology of beliefs, values and characteristics that sustain white supremacy within society."[10] It is an automatic and normative standard from which all other groups are evaluated and deemed unworthy.[11] Ta-Nehisi Coates describes Whiteness as "an existential danger to the country and the world." This is because Whiteness works invisibly, in covert and overt ways.[12] It is baked into our social norms; it is grounded in our institutional practices, and it is affirmed in nearly every aspect of our daily lives. The effects of Whiteness are all-encompassing and omnipresent.[13]

For Black college students, mediating Whiteness can be particularly difficult and psychologically challenging. They are not immune to the violent history Black people have endured from those advancing White normativity while denouncing Black people as aberrant. Across our campuses today, we see evidence of Black students negotiating their relationship to Whiteness, struggling to reject its inherent premise of their racial inferiority while simultaneously striving to accrue any and all of its tangible protections, privileges, and promises.

White women, too, must negotiate their relationship with Whiteness, particularly as it is implicated in relationship building with young Black women. There is a growing body of literature that supports our understanding of how Whiteness can interfere with honest cross-racial communications between women. According to Zeus Leonardo, the common characteristics of Whiteness include "a) an unwillingness to name the contours of racism, b) the avoidance of identifying with a racial experience or group, . . . and c) the minimization of (this nation's) racist legacy."[14] Increasingly, social scientists are explicating how Whiteness encourages White women to uphold racist systems, and what they can do, if they so choose, to interrupt its effects.[15] One way that Whiteness insinuates itself into the mentoring process can be traced back to the training White women receive in their preparation for counseling work. As each professional area has become increasingly feminized, Elizabeth McKenney argues that the research literature and intervention models relied upon to prepare counselors in social, clinical, and educational psychology are generally oriented to the norms of middle-class, gender-normative White women. Blind adherence to those norms with its avoidance of explicit race talk and its devaluation of the knowledge needed to disrupt historically engrained patterns of race and gender discrimination undermines efforts to engage effectively across our differences.[16] McKenny writes that the rationale supporting patriarchal racism privileges White women because they are *not* Black, and then turns around and labels White women as frail and helpless. This bait and switch serves "to justify [White women's] exclusion from social power and, thereby, limits their ability to meaningfully dismantle the privilege they had been accorded. . . . Thus, White women's socialization has been intentionally confining, in as much an effort to uphold racism as to uphold patriarchy."[17]

And this is where resistance is critical. We seek to join with White mentors in building our collective capacities for effective resistance. The much-needed struggle would be directed against internalizing the systems of Whiteness and patriarchy. For Black women, the resistance is against all that fosters internalized inferiority and self-alienation. For White women, the resistance would call her to refuse "internalizing dominance" and a sense that in her superiority she knows best. Following this path, White mentors can increase their self-awareness, develop their skills to detect oppression in its many forms, and learn how oppression works for some and against other groups of people, depending on their positions in society.

We know there are people who argue that White women will struggle mightily with the tasks we lay out. Some complain that White women, even those who call themselves feminists, have a long, sorry history of calling for gender solidarity but then choosing to ignore the breadth of issues affecting Black and other women with stigmatized identities (e.g., women of color, trans women, gender nonbinary, poor women, large-bodied women, and women with disabilities). That is not solidarity, and it is certainly not a history we wish to repeat. Mimi Schippers argues that "if we claim that racial and ethnic minority femininities are subordinate to White femininity, we obscure the subordination of White women in the gender order and we deny that racialized femininities might actually empower racial and ethnic minority women in a way that White femininities do not for White women."[18] We call for solidarity around the idea that to save ourselves, we must join as sisters and we both must resist. At a very basic level, resistance demands first a recognition that women experience oppression in a wide range of limitations, disadvantages, and disapprovals based on gender. Gender oppression works against women by seeing them as unequal to men and allowing individuals, institutions, and cultural practices to routinely discriminate against women while benefiting men.[19] But as Kimberlé Crenshaw reminds us, "all inequality is not created equal."[20] Long-standing, compounding inequities ultimately lead to woefully unequal social trajectories not of our making.

We invite White mentors to join with Black women as we unite to create a new and intentional mentoring practice. This collaborative undertaking has the power to upend the shortcomings of the traditional colorblind and unidimensional mentoring commonly seen in colleges today. Our hope is for the establishment of quality mentoring relationships between Black and White women that will embrace our multiple dimensions of differences in ways that make us stronger and wiser as we call out the systems of oppression that hold us both down.

Why Resistance for White Women?

Adrienne Rich defines *patriarchy* as follows: "Patriarchy is the power of the fathers: a familial-social, ideological, political system in which men—by force, direct pressure, or through ritual, law, and language, customs, etiquette, education, and the division of labor, determine what part women shall or shall not play, and in which the female is everywhere subsumed under the male."[21] All of us, White women and women of color, have been raised within and trained into a heterosexist patriarchy passed down across generations. Despite our cultural differences, we recognize the familiarity in our respective socialization experiences and see similarities in the messages we received as girls about gender identity, gender roles, and gender expectations. Due to the ubiquitous transmission of these femininity edicts, women have internalized messages about how they and other women ought to look, behave, think, and feel.

Scholars argue that femininity is a social construct that relies on a binary gender system that elevates the status of men and masculinity over the stereotypic attributes, characteristics, and qualities of women. Socially defined traits such as gentleness, caring, selflessness, and humility are upheld as attributes women should aspire to and adopt as their own. Many of these traits are influenced by social and cultural factors and thus can vary across individuals, societies, class, and cultural groups. Nonetheless, from childhood through adolescence and adulthood, these messages are woven into the fabric of society—in the family, the media, religions, educational systems, and our consumer culture. Everywhere we turn, traditional binary gender norms prevail, and notions of mainstream femininity are generally upheld and reinforced.

Many of us have learned of the subtle ways in which womanhood is devalued within the United States and in other patriarchal nations around the globe. Conventional attitudes to femininity contribute to the subordination of women. For gender nonconforming women, traditional beliefs about gender acceptability can be particularly treacherous to navigate. Under patriarchy, individuals who identify outside of the conventional gender and sexual binary are frequently demeaned, devalued, and sometimes violently acted against. Cisgender women find that conventional notions about femininity can be used against them too. Despite patriarchal values that sanction women's compliance, dependence, and vulnerability, women, even those who demonstrate gender normative identities, are often penalized when they adopt these values.[22] The women who dare to challenge gender norms can find themselves treading wearily through innumerable stereotypes. Women are still perceived to be weaker. Women are still assumed to lack physical strength and the intellectual agility needed for governing with a level head and a steady hand. Arguably, some of these attitudes are scrutinized and debated; nonetheless, the aforementioned qualities are most often associated with men.

There are many traditional ideas about gender that are experienced as emotionally stifling and that hamper healthy social and psychological development. Some women acquiesce to these normative forces, whereas some choose to free themselves from the dictates of others. Those are the women who resist. We've seen White women do so in ways that are quiet and behind the scenes, while others adopt life changes that are more visible, bravely bodacious and profound.[23] Building on the work of the pioneering Black women in the Combahee River Collective, our model of *intersectional resistance* calls for White mentors and Black mentees to resist together in solidarity.[24] We do this with an acute awareness of the persisting gender and racial inequalities facing us, refusing to accept the assaults perpetrated against any and all of our identities—whether they are identities we come into the world with or those we may choose or change along the way.

To illustrate the importance of resistance in the lives of White women, our discussion begins with a focus on three socializing messages. These are messages that most of us, regardless of race and ethnicity, commonly receive while coming of age in the United States and in other societies. These messages are (1) niceness regulation, (2) external validation, and (3) body policing. We chose these three culturally informed beliefs and practices to highlight their pervasiveness. We remind the reader of two important facts. First, differences in gender identity, race, class, age, and physical appearance structure how we relate to gendered expectations in our lives. There is no universal way to be a woman, and how we are socially positioned speaks volumes about how we uphold or resist notions of womanhood. Second, women's vulnerability is increased when they choose to oppose the dominant messages about traditional gender role attitudes and behavioral expectations. Stepping outside of the boundaries of what is generally considered appropriate, acceptable, or desirable can result in a wide range of retaliatory responses.

We invite White women to think about these matters from a racially informed perspective—one that foregrounds Whiteness in particular, as well as traditional female and middle-class gender roles and identities. We want White women to realize that their race and gendered identities and experiences are interconnected. It is our experience that many White women minimize the personal relevance of race and perceive themselves to be raceless. For many Black mentees, race is salient in the socialization messages they received about womanhood and was reinforced throughout their lives. Although it might be hard to hear, we strongly urge White female mentors to appreciate that some Black mentees will see you primarily as White people who are women and not as women who happen to be White.

Niceness Regulation

Women live beneath an unrelenting social gaze, pressured with cultural expectations that mandate unrelenting likeability. Being a "nice girl" conveys patriarchal expectations of female compliance, self-silence, and unwavering cooperativeness. Women, in this point of view, should not create waves, nor should they cause discomfort to others by being opinionated and disagreeable. We have all heard these messages in one way or another. Thankfully, not all women comply with these expectations;

many of us refuse them forcefully. But women who do not comply resist at their own peril. They are often deemed difficult, man-hating, and radical, ultimately accused of being unfeminine. Their sexuality is questioned.

The social mandate to be nice is one that expects women to defer to others in order to be judged as collaborative and caring. This puts women in the self-sacrificing trap of putting the needs of everyone else, particularly men and children, above their own. When the focus is on gaining approval and avoiding rejection, self-care is akin to being selfish. Even the act of contemplating whether one can say no can make some women feel like they are failing others. And then when they feel they have let people down, the guilt and shame can be overwhelming. Denying help to others who are in need puts women in a moral quandary; their inability to serve selflessly is a miscarriage of femininity and a denial of the dictates of gender roles and norms of behavior. Moreover, it is seen as an insult to decency, the family, God, and the stability of social order.

Nice women may appear to be accepted, but in many circles women who acquiesce to norms of niceness above all else are easily dismissed. Of course, not all women feel the need to be nice in order to be accepted. Individual women are free to make individual decisions, and thankfully there are those who contest such narrowly defined social pressures. Yet the need for approval is very real for the women who have close proximity to a mandate of niceness. We call attention to the need for women to resist feeling that they must always be nice and seek social approval. Niceness primes women to say what they perceive others want to hear, whether it actually reflects how they truly feel or matches their inner desires.[25]

When we look at the situation with a racialized lens, we see that White women are marginalized by patriarchy in very particular ways, and sometimes they are complicit in it. Heather Laine Talley argues that "patriarchy seeds a deep fear of conflict in women. Breeding fear of conflict is a tried-and-true strategy for keeping women in line."[26] The "tyranny of nice and kind" leads women and girls to vent the pent-up anger they feel in passive-aggressive, backstabbing, dishonest, and self-loathing ways.[27] Failing to learn how to express one's wants, needs, and honest opinions is fuel for resentment and insecurity. Yet we see many women perpetuating this gender stereotype, wearing the mask while holding other women accountable for doing the same.

Niceness regulation contributes to a burden Black women bear in their efforts to talk with White women openly about racial matters. However, as DiAngelo reminds us, "Niceness is not anti-racism. Niceness is not courageous . . . and it isn't going to get racism on the table—or keep it on the table."[28] Cross-racial mentoring necessarily requires that women engage in race talk, and venturing into this area of discourse can be uncomfortable and frightening, especially for White mentors. Monitoring one's behavior out of the desire to avoid igniting White fragility or holding back out of fear of breeding conflict does neither woman any good, nor does it aid the work both women must do together.[29] Within the context of a mentoring relationship, this "lady-like nice girl" fear of conflict can have adverse consequences for the Black female college student. For example, let's say that a Black student brings to her mentor an experience with racial discrimination. This is not the time for the mentor to retreat behind a veneer of niceness and avoid the disquiet of racism. Nor is it the time for the mentor to invalidate the student's feelings or ignore investigating the accused offender out of a sense of fear. Naming and pushing back against racial bias on campus runs counter to what it means to be a good White woman when being so is presumed to demand silence about race and the avoidance of racial conflict. White mentors' vulnerability is heightened when fearing that their resistance will have adverse consequences, including being alone, isolated, powerless, judged, and unloved. Black women learned long ago that there are moments when the need to resist is undeniable and inescapable. And that resistance may neither look nor sound very nice. In the words of the great abolitionist Frederick Douglass in 1857, "Power concedes nothing without a demand. It never did and it never will." Freedom-fighting troublemakers like Harriet Tubman, Sojourner Truth, Ida B. Wells, Rosa Parks, Angela Davis, and countless unsung others rejected being nice girls. They were morally compelled to disrupt social injustice. White women's stories of antiracism do exist, and many more are being uncovered by historians and memoirists today. Then and now, Black women need White allies who are willing to join in the struggle.[30] White women need Black women who are willing to collaborate in the ongoing work of resistance.

External Validation

A second force that requires intersectional women's resistance is what we are calling *external validation*. External validation occurs when a person internalizes the ideas, beliefs, norms, or voices of others without critical examination or interrogation of what they are accepting as "truth." This behavior is commonly associated with the internalization of authorities external to the self. This process may be unconscious or invisible to the woman herself. Women in the Western world are often socialized to elevate the judgments of others in authority above their own. Evaluations of their ideas and personal choices function to control women's voices and limit their agency. When caught in this quagmire, many women focus on maintaining appearances and upholding the status quo. They walk the party line. They adhere to ideological beliefs embedded in patriarchy and Whiteness. Some women endorse these beliefs to maintain cultural, financial, economic, and social safety. For others, it may be a way to manage the anxiety they experience when departing from heteronormative gender norms. Patriarchy positions White women according to values assigned to body size, sexuality, gender, ethnicity, social class, or religion. Due to this dynamic, some women may not be able to reap the full benefits bestowed upon other women who uphold patriarchy and Whiteness. However, women who are less close to the ideals of womanhood created by patriarchy may actually be at an advantage. They may see the necessity of resistance for their very survival.

Beginning in childhood and accelerating throughout adolescence, girls learn to see themselves through a heterosexual male lens of affirmation. Women's body size, dress and appearance, language usage, and demeanor are carefully monitored for adherence to gender conformity and masculinity validation. When they are frequently told by others what they want, think, believe, or should do, it becomes easier for women to perceive those voices as having more clout and legitimacy. Under these conditions, women demean themselves for having wants or desires that seem to differ from others who clearly know better than they do. This burden to be selfless, to censor oneself, and to contort one's body and mind to refrain from disappointing others contributes to a loss of self. Working overtime to be in perfect alignment and feeling that one must always get it right contributes to depression, anxiety, and disordered eating, which have become rampant among women across race and class.[31]

There is a gatekeeping quality to external validation as power accompanies those who monitor adherence to it. Heather Laine Talley argues that "one effect of patriarchy is that women have a complicated relationship with power, which leads to regularly denying, ignoring, and downplaying how much power we hold."[32] Women in a gatekeeping role seek to receive the residual benefits that status quo adherence might accrue. These women create and maintain barriers that protect those inside the system, even if this means making life miserable for the women cast aside. We see it when White women choose to consistently privilege the perspectives of White people over the perspectives of BIPOC peoples. We see it when White women prop up conventional understandings to invalidate others or when they rationalize and defend racial framings of the way the world should work in order to maintain the social order. "If it's White, it's right" is the internalized mantra repeatedly affirmed and acted upon. External validation can be particularly pernicious because it leads many women to downplay systems of oppression, disavow their own power to resist its effects, and protect Whiteness at all costs. Even when patriarchy tries to remove White women's rights, Whiteness is still upheld and retained for White women. For these reasons, the resistance we invite White women to adopt includes strategies that beckon a high degree of self-reflection at the personal level and at the level of an individual woman's identification with her racial group membership.

The gendered nature of White women's racial identities, reproduced "by repetition and ritual embedded in inequitable power structures," is tough to acknowledge and even harder to dismantle.[33] Shaking loose from these stifling power structures calls for White women to engage in deep reflection about what it means to be White and to ask themselves, "How do I feel about what I discovered? And to whom might I turn to discuss what I have learned?" That is an initial step toward challenging the authority of dominant ideologies and their exercise of unjust power in our lives.

Body Policing

As the saying goes, women are valued for how they look; men are valued for what they do. The specifics differ due to cultural differences in social class, religion, age, and gender identity, but women worldwide tend to be judged by their appearance. Most cisgendered women who are female-bodied are encouraged to use their bodies to perform femininity despite the fact that beauty ideals are restrictive, unrealistic, and often unhealthy. In our femininity performances, we reproduce and define the traditional categories of sex and/or gender. *Body policing* is using inappropriate negative statements and attributions toward other individuals based on their weight or their body size. In Western cultures, we are bombarded with media messages, both from the multibillion-dollar diet industry and from other women, who suggest that our bodies are sites of deficiencies, are inadequate, and are not good enough the way they are. The message is transmitted that something about our bodies should be changed and made better.

Both men and women police women's bodies. All around us, women are shamed for being fat, skinny, tall, short, flat-chested, busty, too plain, and too sexy. We judge ourselves and each other against impossible standards about what the "right" body should look like: taut, thin, and forever young. We compare and criticize women behind their backs and to their faces. Being overweight in particular is seen as constituting a moral failure, and public scrutiny is payback for women daring to partake of what they want and having the audacity to sanction their desires. The meanings we ascribe to underweight women are similarly weighted with social and moral significations—ranging widely from being seen as holding high social status and exhibiting moral virtue to being pitifully self-destructive, consumed by obsessive self-denial and disordered eating.

Body policing is deeply felt, emotionally and psychologically. The wounds that such shaming inflict—lowered self-esteem, the denial of self, a diminished ability to be intimate or vulnerable with others—are all by products of gender oppression. Whether we are shaming one another or shaming ourselves, we wastefully expend our energy fighting the discomfort of someone else's judgment of how we should look or who we should be.

Moreover, body shaming does double duty. It upholds sexism and *misogynoir* (the targeted hatred of Black women) as it props up patriarchal structures by proclaiming the physical characteristics of White women's appearance as an embodiment of beauty standards for everyone.[34] Straight European hair and light skin color are seen as preferred, attractive, and desirable, while darker skin color, coily African hair, and lips that are naturally thick are outside of conventional assumptions of what looks good. Policing women's bodies, especially when it is done by other women, is an example of how women collude in producing and reproducing gender-based social inequalities. Body shaming is designed to keep women insecure, fearing their own choices, and doubting their judgment. Disconnected from our bodies and from our ability to trust our own needs, as well as those of other women, body policing practices distort our ability to see each other in ways that are honest, caring, and nonjudgmental.

Here we have noted three negative normative forces (niceness regulation, external validation, and body policing) of shared concern for women inclusive of their diversity. Just like Black women, White women have much to push back against and resist. As we see it, loving your body regardless of its shape, size, color, or gender expression is an act of resistance in a culture where body shaming is the norm. Learning to lovingly embrace how our different bodies present to the world is in itself an act of resistance. When we own these realities and dismiss the idea that how we look is indicative of a woman's intrinsic value, we refute historically rooted prescriptions that were designed to separate women, place us in a social hierarchy, and pit us against each other. Niceness regulation, external validation, and body policing are just three of the many noxious messages internalized by women in our society. Each of us has our own way of relating to these messages, and how we accept or resist their influence is largely shaped by our racial status and other intersecting social identities. We assert that women will be better able to connect across our differences when we figure out how to release ourselves from being held hostage by fear and insecurity. Resistance is demanded of women who refuse to be silenced and ignored, defined by others, or told to stay in their place. How we resist as White women and as women of color will differ, largely because of the compounding effects of race inequality and discrimination. However, the point here is that all of us have similar resistance-building work to do, and we must do this work together. The work starts with an appreciation of the need for intersectional resistance—an acknowledgment that a Black mentee's resistance may not be the same as a White mentor's resistance but that both groups of women have plenty to stand up to and a great deal to take a stand for. This is a call for White mentors to identify and tap the resources of their own experiences with resistance to connect to their Black mentees' need to do the same. Together they can create a mentoring practice that allows them to co-construct culturally specific resistance strategies that effectively address the social and political contexts of Black female students in college life.

Relational Consequences for Women's Gender Oppression

It is important that we name the elephant in the room. Despite the current attention to race in our national discourse, Black and White women continue to confront a host of difficulties when talking about race with each other. The unequal value placed on the differences in Black and White women's racial statuses is a major reason that these conversations are difficult to have. Black women occupy a socially constructed subordinate position, irrespective of their psychological health and their ability to optimally resist aspects of their oppression. Racial identity holds meanings of historical and contemporaneous significance and elicits personal and cultural pride for Black people. Racial identity for many White women, on the other hand, often has little meaning. White people have been socialized to define themselves by identities of oppression—that is, to be White is to be "not Black"—and it generally doesn't signify much else. As a result, Black people's survival has always required in-depth knowledge of the people and systems that dominate, far deeper knowledge than dominating groups have of themselves.

African Americans have had a very long history of talking about race, racial identity, race relations, and racism. Intraracially, people are considerably more comfortable with these topics. When White people have limited racial literacy, they tend to be less comfortable discussing race and racism. For White mentors who have been socialized into an uncritical acceptance of White supremacist values and beliefs, acknowledging racial difference in a cross-racial relationship can heighten anxiety. Social scientists have shown us that a basic tenet of Whiteness is the belief that race does not matter in interracial relationships. The preference is to stay silent about race and to project a color-evasive stance in order to manage one's image as being fair, multiculturally open, and nonracist.[35]

The cultural cloak of colorblindness is neatly stitched together by ignorance and racial silence. A White mentor can take comfort in the expectation that if race must be addressed in conversation, it is the responsibility of the Black student to initiate the discussion. A shared belief among White people that they are not responsible for being informed about racism can contribute to their inattentiveness to race matters. Relying on Black students who may be traumatized by racism to "pull it together" and teach their White mentors is a dereliction of duty and a self-serving form of psychological abandonment. This erroneous belief that race only resides in non-White bodies relieves White people from awareness, accountability, and culpability. Holding onto these beliefs also relieves White people from bearing the massive burden of race, transferring the responsibility instead to their young Black mentees. Staying silent about race, whether out of a sense of fear or due to not wanting to break rank with other White people or due to concerns that such conversations might cause conflict with a Black mentee, relieves White mentors of seeing racism as a relationship in which both groups are involved.[36]

Some White women avoid "race talk" because it makes them uncomfortable. They grew up learning that good women did not talk about race, sex, religion, or politics, or they may have been raised in neighborhoods with few non-White people. Limited practice in talking about race with Black people is a consequence of Whiteness, and the perpetuation of race silence is the ultimate assertion of White privilege and power. Whether, when, and with whom to talk openly about race is complicated. It is easy to understand why such conversations are thought best left alone.

Because we know that White people will face life challenges and roadblocks, but systematic racism will not be one of them, many White women who are assigned to cross-racial mentoring relationships may need special preparation for dealing with racism's effects. Systematic racism is an unrelenting problem for Black women on college campuses, requiring full attention and caring concern. The degree to which their mentors are able, willing, and prepared to battle gendered racism alongside their students of color can make a tremendous difference in the effectiveness and safety of their relationship. Developing the ability to critique one's socialization into White supremacy and patriarchy is essential preparation for White women's resistance. Understanding the hurdles to overcome when communicating with Black women is equally important. Interrogating these patterns will allow White mentors to hear their Black students with clarity and respond with honesty and without fear. The mentor will also need to join with her mentee in creating effective resistance strategies.

Finally, White women's communication across differences can be hampered by being too quick to assert the primacy of gender inequality above all other oppressions. This "race to innocence" can be a distortion of the social and political realities that women navigate in a culturally diverse society.[37] Being thoughtful about how oppression operates means recognizing the wide array of challenges that diverse women confront. We must all remember that feeling oneself marginalized in one dimension of identity does not negate the privilege and advantage a woman receives in other life domains.

Managing Racial Emotions in Mentoring Relationships

Letting go of the silence and daring to speak honestly about racial matters with other women across differences can be a particularly anxiety-provoking experience for White women. In her book *White Fragility*, Robin DiAngelo argues that White women must resist the defensiveness of White fragility in the face of racial discomfort. She defines *White fragility* as "a state in which even a minimal amount of racial stress in the habitus becomes intolerable, triggering a range of defensive moves."[38] The moves she refers to, and which we agree that White women must resist, include the racialized emotions of guilt, denial, shame, and fear. DiAngelo argues that White fragility is about social control. Tears, whether they flow from a sense of guilt and sadness or from frustration, anger, and righteous indignation, can function as weapons and serve to hold Black women hostage.[39] White women's tears keep Black women and other women of color in their place by bullying them from a position of vulnerability. In turn, BIPOC women subordinate their own needs while taking care of their emotionally needy White female counterparts. The irony is that White women, exploiting their femininity by behaving frail, summon men and some women to their aid. This emotional blackmail derails relational connectivity, engenders resentment and distrust, and ultimately denies Black women the expression of honest human emotions they may be feeling in the moment.

Patriarchy and Whiteness undermine the ability for women to build or to repair ruptures in cross-racial relationships. Thus, in preparing for the work of intentional mentoring, we encourage White women to resist suppressing discomfort from unsettling race-based emotions. We respect that these affective states generally coexist with the disquieting racial knowledge that White mentors may be grappling with. Seeking to eradicate these emotions is not realistic, but decreasing the fear and anxiety evoked from them is possible. What we hope is that these emotions can be effectively managed so that the work of relationship building can be sustained.

When White mentors resist the compulsion to center their White racial comfort, they become better able to see the strengths of Black women, while gaining a broader historical and racial sense of themselves. In the four hundred years since Black Africans arrived on these shores, Black women have, out of necessity, been forced to manage and monitor the ins and outs of White fragility: they have learned how to recognize it and not incite its fury. Black women have long realized that the system was designed to elevate White women's status over their own. On the other hand, White women have never been free of the negating forces of patriarchy and White (male) supremacy. The trap does not look the same, but both groups of women find themselves caught in its snare.

This discussion is, at first blush, an exploration of what Black women need to build healthy and effective resistance in the college years. But it is also a call to White women, our Sister Resisters, to build their own capacities for resistance against those who would diminish their humanity. Women of African descent have had to wage this fight against sexism and racism and have done so alone or with other Black women. To do justice to history, there have been times when White women have joined in solidarity with Black women to push back, together, against the joint tyrannies of racism and sexism. Now is the time for us to join forces again—to learn from each other and develop the capacity for connection that is achieved through empathy, memory, and experience.

Filling the Knowledge Gap

A basic principle in all professional development that focuses on diversity training, antiracism, multicultural sensitivity, and the promotion of culturally responsive pedagogy is the belief that it is the responsibility of the teacher, counselor, and mentor to educate herself about the students who she serves. Fortunately, White mentors have a great deal of material available to educate them about the Black women on their college campuses. There is a considerable amount of historical, social, and political scholarship that can aid White mentors as they seek to work effectively with this population. Throughout this book, we integrate some of this social knowledge. By calling attention to the attitudes and affects mentors need to enhance their cross-racial relational connections, we hope to guide mentors in their efforts to build strong mentoring relationships. We advocate for the acquisition of skills that are required for Black and White women to hear each other, appreciate their diverse sociopolitical contexts, and respect their differing racialized perspectives. Inevitably, blind spots exist. We hold this reality and seek to suspend judgement, honoring what women have had to do to survive racialized gender oppression and recognizing each other's unseen and closeted strengths.

Facilitating Relational Knowledge

We have identified critical knowledge that we believe White mentors need to be aware of and apply in their work with Black female mentees. Appreciating the diversity within Black student populations, their specific cultural histories in this nation, and their experiences with race and racism are key. There is ongoing personal work that mentors need to do. This includes developing racial knowledge, being critically aware of their unearned privileges, and being able to locate their proximity to the perpetuation of systemic inequality. The mentors' clarity about and appropriate uses of their power are essential to the cultivation of trust in mentoring relationships.

Diasporic Black History

How many of us truly know the cultural backgrounds of the Black students enrolled in our colleges or universities? Many of us who were educated in American schools need to fill in the gaps that exist between the history taught to most Americans and the histories of African peoples. Those histories were distorted, Whitewashed, or willfully forgotten over time. African American history *is* US history. It tells a different and more complex story of who we are as a people and of our shared destiny. Similarly, because many of our colleges and universities are filled with women of African descent from other areas of the globe—Afro-Caribbean, African nationals, and multiple other regions in the world—it is just as important to have a sense of the life trajectories and immigration histories of these women and their families.

Recognition of Black Multiethnicity

There are Americans from all groups who still mistakenly assume that Black people are a monolith. Nothing can be further from the truth. According to a recent study by the Pew Research Center, "More than 46 million people in the US self-identified as Black in 2019, representing a 29 percent increase from 2000, and making up 14 percent of the country's population. And while single race Black people who don't identify as Hispanic accounted for 87 percent of the US Black population in 2019, multiracial Black and Hispanic Black groups, both young and rapidly expanding populations, have each grown by more than 140 percent since 2000."[40] Clearly, Black people are multiethnic, with very different histories and immigration statuses. Ten percent of Black people living in the United States today are immigrants. Knowing how Black people are socially positioned sharpens our understanding of the contemporary issues they may be facing across life domains. Failure to recognize these important intraracial differentiations can lead to Black college students feeling misunderstood, overlooked, and that their needs are irrelevant.

Experiences with Race and Racism

Black women, including college students, tend to have much more in-depth knowledge of how race works in institutions and in society than their White peers and mentors. The reverse is not often the case. White women generally do not need to understand and appreciate Black women's experiences in the same way in which Black women must understand and appreciate White women's experiences. Indeed, under systems of Whiteness and niceness, White women are discouraged from doing so. Understanding the impact of racialized experiences, including those that have been positive and those that have been negative in the lives of Black college student mentees, is fundamental. To provide the best support to her mentee, it is imperative that the mentor have an awareness of the barriers and of the resources in the mentee's life. Open and honest communication between mentors and mentees goes a long way toward filling this knowledge gap.

The Development of White Mentors' Racial Knowledge

The history of Whiteness in America tells us that there were many White people creating White identities that were deliberately constructed to subjugate and annihilate others. To this day, there are those who continue to celebrate White identities that perpetuate such inequities. Both historically and now, some White women, including those who identify as feminists, marginalize BIPOC women even within social justice movements. We hope that White mentors will use this awareness to recognize that privileged racial status secures advantages for some at a cost to others. This information is necessary for acquiring the racialized self-knowledge needed to build caring and productive relationships across our differences. Knowing one's racial history, warts and all, is a non-negotiable, albeit uncomfortable, step women must take in the journey to "know themselves."[41]

Acknowledging One's Unearned Privileges

Scholars have referred to unearned White skin privilege as the *wages of Whiteness*—a payment in the form of social status.[42] Ignoring these unearned privileges and how they shape the lives of individuals contributes to women being unable to see their own complicity in the system of Whiteness. Being awake to how privilege advantages White women while disadvantaging their Black sisters encourages the creation of bonds that are mutual, respectful, and reciprocal.[43] Unpacking that knapsack of unearned privileges continues to be a worthwhile and productive exercise for White mentors. It expands their understanding of the invisible systems that confer dominance on those with White skin color.[44]

Recognizing One's Proximity to Systems of Inequality

Social scientists have long argued that all of us, Black, White, Latinx, Asian, gender nonconforming, and all other minoritized groups need to know that even if we are not actively resisting racism, none of us are immune from its systems of bias and discrimination. We are all impacted by racism's toxicity. It is in the air we breathe, and it is part and parcel of nearly all of the processes and procedures of every institution in our nation. Our silence will not save us. Resisting racial oppression is everyone's business, and within cross-racial mentoring relationships, it is vital and empowering.

Understanding Power and Developing Relational Trust

As Jernigan et al. explain, "White people who embody a healthy and sophisticated racial consciousness are aware of racial systems of privilege; they are able to discuss racism, and they recognize how racism affects them personally. And, most importantly, they act in an effort to combat racial discrimination."[45] Knowledge gaps among White mentors may provide valuable information for professionals who are designing mentoring practices. It is our fervent hope that White women self-educate regarding the sexism in their lives. Moreover, this knowledge can be used to challenge gendered racism in their work with Black women. Ultimately, we want White mentors to be actively engaged and physically present in this work. We hope that they will share with their mentees what they have learned from their own lived experiences struggling against whatever oppression they've had to confront. Sister Resisters who take personal responsibility for building a meaningful relationship recognize that there might be moments of hesitation and mistrust. Despite these concerns, they can demonstrate to their mentees a commitment to their work together. At the heart of that work is an ethic of caring that manifests in sustained *race talk*—conversations that facilitate cross-racial communication.

In this chapter, we provided foundational knowledge regarding the relevance of resistance for White mentors in their work with Black mentees. Talking about racism only goes so far. Our model encourages active resistance. As you read subsequent chapters, we ask you to reflect on how you might improve your readiness as a brave, well-informed, and responsible Sister Resister united against injustice with Black female college students.

FUNDAMENTALS FOR SISTER RESISTER MENTORS

To end this chapter, we present a list of fundamentals that we invite mentors to consider as they further develop their roles as effective resisters.

- If you are in the academy, think about whose books you review, whose promotions you write for, and what committees you serve on.
- Reflect on who you consider to be the White allies in your life. Do you assume there are only so many seats at the antiracist table? How can you elongate the table?
- Be mindful of your language. Respect that we live in a global context that is fluid and ever-changing. Be open to these changes reflected in language use—especially related to how people wish to self-identify racially and according to their gender identity.
- Think about how you hold your body with the people you work with. What does your body communicate to your White colleagues? To BIPOC? What might that awareness reveal?
- Turn the world map upside down: Global South at the top, Global North at the bottom. Know that White people are the numerical minority, only one-eighth of the world's population.

- Search for your mother's rebellious gardens.
- Read essential works about White Sister Resisters: *My Mama's Dead Squirrel* (Mab Segrest); *Yours in Struggle: Three Perspectives on Antisemitism and Racism* (Elly Bulkin, Minnie Bruce Pratt, and Barbara Smith); *Blood, Bread and Poetry* (Adrienne Rich); *Blue Front* (Martha Collins); *White Women, Race Matters* (Ruth Frankenberg). Keep current. Build on the experiences of White Sister Resisters before you.
- Seek out Black culture, books, art, history, and music. Be aware of essential books for Sister Resisters: *The Souls of Black Folk* (W. E. B. Du Bois); *The Alchemy of Race and Rights: Diary of a Law Professor* (Patricia J. Williams); *Home Girls: A Black Feminist Anthology* (Barbara Smith); *Sister Outsider* (Audre Lorde); *Beloved, The Bluest Eye*, and *Source of Self Regard* (Toni Morrison); *Wayward Lives, Beautiful Experiments: Intimate Histories of Riotous Black Girls, Troublesome Women and Queer Radicals* (Saidaya Hartman); *Black on Both Sides: A Racial History* (C. Riley Snorton); *My Grandmother's Hands* (Resmaa Menakem); *Go Tell It on The Mountain* (James Baldwin), *Pedagogies of Crossings* (M. Jacqui Alexander); *Me and White Supremacy* (Layla Saad); *Between the World and Me* (Ta-Nehisi Coates). Don't stop here; there are so many others you should seek out and read.
- Know the history of slavery and/or settler colonialism in your own family's history.
- Know the distinct history of Black women globally. Haiti was the first country in the Western Hemisphere to abolish slavery. Ethiopia is a country in Africa that was never colonized. Women are at the heart of anticolonial, antislavery struggles. Black lesbians are at the forefront of liberation struggles across the globe.
- Consider where you worship, shop, vacation, live, and send your children to school or camp. Perhaps shifts are needed in your life. Seek out integrated spaces.
- Listen to Black women. Their perspectives come from generations of resistance. If they are willing to share their stories in your presence, this may signal safety and trust. Don't center yourself in their stories.

- Show up at demonstrations with your mentees. Watch your consciousness expand.
- Speak up because it is the right thing to do even when there are no Black people there to validate you.
- Know that cultural humility includes making mistakes, making amends, and committing to learning more. Guilt is a way station with no train leading in or out.
- Recognize and honor that oppression breeds resistance.
- Know that a few doors will close, but the whole world opens up. Lift a toast.[46]

CHAPTER 3

Sister Resisters and the Work of Meaningful Mentoring

THE COMEDIAN CHRIS ROCK made famous the following observation: "All my Black friends have a bunch of White friends. And all my White friends have *one* Black friend." Unfortunately, his perception is confirmed by scholarly research. According to a report issued by the Public Religion Research Institute, for every ninety-one White friends a White American has, they only have one Black friend. The study also found that 75 percent of Whites have "entirely White social networks without any minority presence."[1] Income inequality, residential segregation, religious differences, political polarization, and our tendency to seek out and associate with people who are similar to us help to explain why, for the vast majority of Americans, close and ongoing cross-racial interactions are shockingly rare.[2]

Recently, a colleague employed in a large public university shared this mentoring story with us. A small program in one of the colleges in the university set up a mentoring program, matching faculty and staff with sophomore undergraduates. Because the program was deemed successful (i.e., it ended after fourteen weeks with the same number of students it began with), an administrator made the decision to "scale up." They put out the order to recruit more students and find more faculty and staff for the program. When my colleague asked about who would train the mentors and what the training would address, she was brushed off and told the program had everything under control. The director felt confident that "everyone knows how important it is for the undergrads to talk about racism, and we'll give them space to do that."

My colleague waited patiently, but quickly became disheartened when she heard very few details from her administrator about how these conversations would take place. Questions swirled regarding who would facilitate the interactions and what the faculty was expected to do with this information. After an unproductive back and forth, the exasperated administrator seemed quick to change the subject. "Faculty will know what to do," she said, anxious to bring the conversation to a close.

When universities establish cross-racial mentoring programs and funding becomes the sole driver of the project, the mission of mentoring is compromised. To be effective, mentors require specialized training, need to be held accountable to the students that they serve, and need to be committed to the ideals of social justice.

Mentoring has developed into a major programmatic activity that faculty, staff, administrators, and others are expected to engage in with students on campus. Some mentoring is formal—usually set up through an organized program or student assignment process. In those cases, the student and staff member may know little about one another prior to their first meeting. Often the challenge in these situations is how to build a relationship if there had been none previously. Other mentoring matchups are more informal; for example, the relationship between the adults and the Black students may previously exist and might already be developing more organically.

Orienting students to a college and socializing them to a particular field or discipline are some of the ways that mentors provide social support and serve as role models to mentees.[3] Because race and gender can deeply influence the mentoring relationship, we know that cross-cultural/cross-racial mentoring relationships are often difficult to sustain.[4] Most challenging to the partnership is how racial realities are talked about (or not). Feeling a lack of safety on the part of either participant can quickly silence or undermine conversations that involve race. We maintain that the mentor's avoidance of race topics impacts the mentee far more than the mentee's silence impacts the mentor. Yet conversations pertaining to race are exactly what Black students say they want and feel they need. At the heart of relational connections is trust and respect between the two women. As a student named Kesha explains:

I want a mentor who will not just offer me advice or tell me that she has my back and is looking out for me, but also really knows me and understands what my experiences at this college look like through my eyes. I want my mentor to be able to listen to me, hear me, and work with me—a Black woman—as I grow and develop—academically, intellectually, emotionally, and socially. I don't want my mentor to ever forget who I am and the racism, sexism, classism, and homophobia that women who look like me face.

A mentor's anxiety can interfere with a productive cross-racial connection. In this racially charged and polarizing political climate, mentors might fear they are perceived as overly privileged, racially ignorant, or, worse yet, racist. Not surprisingly, it can feel daunting to be responsible for imparting knowledge, providing guidance, and offering support to a young woman who neither looks like you nor shares your same background and experiences. But with thoughtful preparation, Sister Resisters can manage their anxiety. They can bring into the mentoring practice a tool kit of resistance skills that will help circumvent relational disconnection.

In our opinion, White women who are able and willing to take up this ongoing project share common characteristics that allow them to be effective with young Black women. They think, act, and emote in ways that reflect how they are engaged in self-work, and they exhibit evidence showing they are culturally informed, particularly about the challenges faced by *all* women in this society. They reject the hierarchical paradigms that drive patriarchy and White supremacy—refusing to believe that one's race or gender is better than all others. To that end, these mentors understand the essential role of psychological, social, and political resistance in the lives of women today.

It's one thing for White women to see the struggles of women of color as solely unique to those women and thus unrelated to White women's lives. It is quite another thing to see our lives connected, our concerns intertwined, and the obstacles we face as emerging from a similar toxic source. Seeing ourselves allied in our resistance allows us to push back collectively against those who would devalue who we are and to stand up together for what is right and fair for us all. Such mentoring can make for a mighty alliance between women (and those who support women), one that acknowledges the unique and the common challenges faced by women coming of age in this society and that builds on our collective capacities to overcome the negative forces of racism, sexism, and other forms of social oppression.

Ultimately, we believe in our power to change one another's lives for good. The skills and talents White mentors bring to relationships can become a dynamic catalyst for Black female students' personal and academic development, particularly when the mentor is culturally knowledgeable, engaged, and purposeful. As Kesha explained earlier, Black female students are looking for relationships on campus with mentors who understand them—as women, as *Black* women, and as Gen Zers and millennials who must utilize multiple bodies of knowledge, skills, and abilities to combat gendered and racial bias. Significant numbers of people shape a Black student's fate on a college campus, and not always for the better. These students are looking to us to help them uncover the unwritten lessons of how women working together can lead lives that are strong, smart, and resourceful. This is what it takes to become Sister Resisters: White female mentors working intentionally in deep and meaningful relationships with Black female students.

Transforming Individually and Together

Earlier, we mentioned that when young adults and their mentors work together, they engage in processes of *reciprocal transformation* in that they have the potential to promote each other's development.[5] We all grow and change with new experiences and through our interactions with people whose backgrounds and previous life experiences are new to us. Dual and interactive developmental processes transpire in both the Black female student and her (usually) White mentor. Critical elements of Black students' identity and social development unfold alongside those elements that are simultaneously unfolding in the mentor. Two key factors are associated with this transformational phenomenon as it relates to building effective mentoring relationships across differences. First, White women mentors and their Black student mentees all have the potential to grow and develop in their attitudes and beliefs about race, class, and gender, albeit from different starting points and progressing at different rates. Both groups of women are co-constructing their own personal identities with knowledge gained through their relational connections. Second, it is important to note that these women, through their interactions with each other, both impact and are impacted by the other.

Higher education institutions have instituted workshops, lectures, courses, and other on-the-job training to better prepare faculty and staff members to work more effectively with an increasingly multicultural student population. Universities rely on diversity training, particularly if they have a mentoring program. However, diversity training can be intermittent, with little follow through after the initial sessions. Moreover, the information provided in these workshops can be overwhelming, emotionally draining, and scary and can contribute to feelings of defensiveness. Even when training is well designed and the participants are open to its message, we all know that training alone is not enough. The fact that there is so much to learn and reflect upon invokes a need for mentors to continually self-educate.

Developing Self-Knowledge

Liz and Tricia's story is one that plays out on campuses across the country.

Liz was excited to participate in the new mentoring program that began in the fall semester at the start of the new year. She was matched with a young Black woman named Tricia, and Liz thought she and Tricia were getting along just fine. They met for coffee once or twice before midterms, and then again a few weeks later. It wasn't until Liz checked in around finals that she learned of Tricia's failing grades in two of her classes. They met one last time at the end of winter break, with Liz offering Tricia a pep talk to launch the new semester. Tricia seemed less animated than she'd been in the fall, but she promised she'd turn things around and would get back on track. As the weeks went on, Tricia dropped out of sight. Even after receiving multiple academic warning letters, Tricia didn't answer Liz's emails or phone calls. Hearing nothing, Liz lost track of her mentee until she was told in May that Tricia decided she wouldn't return to the college for her sophomore year.

Liz was disappointed and confused. *Why didn't Tricia tell me what was going on with her? Was she having money troubles? Did she need a tutor? I thought we were getting along just fine. Why did she shut me out?* Liz spent the summer wondering how she could build better relationships with her Black mentees the next time around.

Working effectively across social differences calls for mentors to attend closely to how our social identities may affect our lives, influencing who we are and how we relate to others on a daily basis. Adolescence is a major developmental period of identity formation; we see this every day in the college students with whom we work. But for most of us, identity-defining experiences, roles, values, and biases continue to influence our development throughout most of our adulthood years. Adult mentors are shaped in their own personal and professional development through the nature of their connections with the young people they teach and support.[6] White women's identities are constructed and interrogated in their relationships with Black female college students. Building strong relationships that honor and respect the identities that both groups of women bring together calls for mentors to engage in self-work.

We have found that many mentors tend to be comfortable thinking about identity formation as exclusive to adolescence. They make the mistake of associating racial identity with being relevant only to people of color. Often, adult mentors have less facility in exploring their multiple identities. Many have not spent much time reflecting on their identities individually or in their totality. As a result, they might be less attuned to how identity evolves and shifts over time. Take, for example, the process experienced by students as they reveal their sexual orientation or gender identity after keeping it a secret from others. While coming out of the closet is typically described as a single and dramatic act, many lesbians experience it as a dynamic, halting, situational, and ongoing process, a series of doors and hallways to navigate throughout one's lifetime. It can be an ongoing challenge to integrate various aspects of the self (i.e., as female, while also being a White female, while also being a White female who is a lesbian).

When mentors pay attention to the interconnected social categories of individual and group differences that we embody, they deepen their understanding of the strengths Black students bring into the classroom. With this knowledge, they gain greater insight into the struggles faced outside the classroom door. Acknowledging the ways difference unfolds in the mentor's life can provide useful tools for self-discovery and skill development, as well as for self-care while caring for others.

So, to be specific, if a professor is an advisor for a student who grew up in Mali and the advisor has not worked with many Malian students before, doing reading and attending talks on the country's ongoing struggles with armed political factions, severe drought, and food insecurity can support a developing relationship between the faculty and mentee. Chances are this student already knows a tremendous amount about US history. It is then on the mentor to do some of the catch-up work. One of the hesitations that White faculty identify about race talk is the worry of prying or asking a cultural question that is too basic or that makes one look ignorant. When White faculty do their own background research, they grow the confidence needed to have genuine conversations about history, culture, and politics. Appreciating the complexities of cultural differences requires time and effort. That said, mentors are not excused in these situations from choosing to not learn. Do not allow your thoughts to get stuck, worrying that "There's just too much to know" or "I just don't know anything," as such rationalizations stymie real connection and conversation.[7]

Those of us who reside in the Western world all grew up breathing in the toxic air of race-based and economic oppression, with its long history of associated systemic and pervasive inequalities. Black students carry with them the weight of this historic marginalization. Inevitably, both mentors and mentees internalize misinformation and stereotypes that shape our understanding of who we are in relationship to one another.

Self-work for White female mentors suggests that they interrogate how their identity statuses may at times connect them to their students while it may at other times create barriers in the relationship. Doing this calls for mentors to explore how Whiteness shapes their self-concept. For instance, we are used to thinking about how our Black female student's background may have been impacted by racial bias and discrimination. But for mentors, understanding one's racial heritage or how your family and your community gained privileges can be an equally important way to appreciate how your racial past influences your current position. This can be an unsettling and critical factor to deeply consider.

Reciprocal transformation is a dynamic process that the mentor and the student experience while growing and learning as individuals, as cultural beings, and as members of this society. This process generates intentional relationships. Such knowledge will bring about change in both directions.

As mentors engage in the self-work that we propose, they will recognize their own implicit biases and how they might distort relationships. Their work with Black female students will become more clear, more purposeful, and more effective. To pursue this work, psychologists suggest that mentors practice *cultural humility*. This term refers to a multifaceted approach to establish strong cross-racial mentoring relationships that include ongoing self-critique. Cultural humility means a commitment to addressing power imbalances in the mentoring relationship. As much as possible, power should be shared with people collaborating with and learning from each other. And mentors should be willing to partner with and advocate on behalf of their mentees.[8] Sustaining meaningful and productive relationships across social differences takes time and intention. There is no roadmap to follow, and there are no easy answers. Despite the challenges, there is the potential for significant evolution in both groups of women as they embrace the reality that there is always so much more to learn.

Contextualizing the Mentoring Space

Students are constantly learning about themselves and their place in the world through what we teach in the classroom and through the interactions they encounter in and outside of the classroom. Roseline, a junior attending a state university, explained, "I grew up with Haitian parents, who fed me plenty of messages about how different we are from Black Americans—and in many ways we are, but when I walk into the student center, the White students look at me as just another Black student taking a scholarship away from them." Although Roseline identifies as Haitian, she contends with dominant discourses regarding Blackness that too often eclipse the defining role of ethnicity among racially similar people. More than that, her sense of racial identity is heightened by how she is perceived and treated in the United States based on racialized beliefs, assumptions, and expectations. Roseline must grapple with seeing herself as different yet the same.

In chapter 1, we discussed the hostile climate on college campuses that Black female students say they must contend with: gendered racial bias, stereotypes, microaggressions, and other cultural insensitivities among students, faculty, and staff. Students complain that they have to withstand racially insensitive attitudes expressed in classrooms and on campus, coupled with race-avoidant behaviors. They perceive the curriculum as Eurocentric, with BIPOC perspectives seldom represented or valued in course materials. Moreover, students tell us of the heightened anxiety they experience while navigating toxic campus climates. They feel the impositions of Whiteness as they walk through the geographical spaces in higher education institutions or attend the formal and informal activities organized on campus that often leave them feeling othered and as though they do not belong.

Traversing these minefields is indeed stressful, yet the hard work that these Black female students engage in is seldom acknowledged, nor is it appreciated by college staff. Instead, we expect our Black students to buck up, be strong, and draw strength from their adversities, while offering them little assistance to do so. The model we present offers a very different response to the burdens shouldered by these young Black women. As Sister Resisters gain a clearer understanding of the developmental journeys unfolding in college for Black female students, they are better able to design intervention strategies that effectively address their needs. Mentors who commit to truly knowing Black students, who understand the paths they have traveled, and who can identify what they are up against are in a better position to be more adept when supporting them in their struggles. For example, a Sister Resister who has a sophisticated understanding of Haitian independence, Haiti's relationship to other Caribbean countries, and the complications of Black identity due to colonialism may be better able to anticipate and problem-solve with a student like Roseline. Adopting an intersectional lens provides us with important tools. We can analyze, apply, and assess our work with Black women in ways that acknowledge and appreciate intersectional dynamics. In doing so, understanding is strengthened between White mentors and Black mentees, which enhances their relational bond.

Knowledge is socially constructed, "rooted in and shaped by particular positions and interests . . . [and] constituted through relations of power."[9] Many Black students enter their institutions having learned to expect struggle and erasure; they have been forewarned and are prepared. Some may become hypervigilant and at times overly sensitive to interpersonal and institutional dynamics that they perceive as racially charged. Others, like Roseline, may have received little advanced warning of how to handle the low expectations of others. They may need help to navigate through the well-documented risks that operate in the classrooms and on the grounds of their own campuses. Sister Resisters pay attention to racial socialization. They seek knowledge and ask the kinds of questions that help them to learn about the messages students received regarding what it means to be Black and female within a global context. In this way, a strong mentor listens with intention for ways to integrate a strengths-based model into her work with Black women. Such a mentor can help Black students to uncover the culturally based strengths they may be bringing to the college environment. These elements can help them to reject deficit thinking and affirm themselves and the journey they are on.

Just as we would never expect a student athlete to perform a dangerous move on the field without the benefit of safety gear, we fail Black female students when we expect them to singularly overcome the multiple risk domains in colleges and universities that hijack their social and academic success.[10] Fortunately, researchers have identified institutional, racial, and ethnic protective factors that foster academic and personal resilience for Black students in higher education. These include race-based organizations and affinity groups on campus, creating interventions that work with same-race peers, and building on racial socialization messages students bring with them to campus.[11] Effective mentors of Black female students are cognizant of the strategies that foster success and know how to effectively implement those practices. This allows us to be better allies and more intentional in our work.

Calling Out Institutional Barriers

We need more mentors who will take the time to educate themselves about systemic inequities on campus and are willing to identify patterns of racial, sexual, gendered, and class-based bias throughout the institution. Moreover, we need mentors who have developed the capacity to take action (alone and with other change agents) to address the inequalities they see on college campuses. There are many ways this can be accomplished. Working with others on campus, faculty, staff, and administrators can develop strategies to identify and dismantle the systems that create barriers for Black students' success. Together they can identify services and programs that support students' needs. If programs do not exist, mentors and their allies can advocate for their creation.

Mentors have the capacity to intervene and be effective in support of Black students in ways that those students perhaps cannot. For example, White mentors can access spaces where students and faculty of color, or other members with stigmatized identities, are excluded or simply tolerated. Finally, mentors can connect Black college women to individuals within networks and supports who share their identities. For example, alumni, individuals from affinity groups, and professional student organizations have Black members who are familiar with the challenges of inclusion. Such guidance paired with cultural understanding is often what Black students need to achieve their career goals. Sister Resisters can work with allies on campus in other ways. For instance, in academic institutions, much gets done informally after faculty meetings, at lunch, and across an array of social contexts. Because faculty and administrators have access to their informal networks, they have tremendous power to reshape conversations with their peers. How often have we heard the comment, "I'm not so sure they are right for this program," from well-meaning faculty talking about cultural fit. Our sense is that it often masks thinly veiled biases regarding which students faculty believe really belong. These are the conversations that can make or break whether students get admitted into programs and receive internships, fellowships, and other positions that are critical to jump-starting their careers. Mentors who are alert to such negating institutional discourses can play a role in interrupting their effect.

Zoe, an assistant dean of students, was thrilled to be asked to head up the new mentoring program for communication majors in her college. She saw this as an opportunity to provide extra guidance to students, the kind she had needed years ago. While in college, Zoe's family dealt with her brother's heroin addiction. During that time, Zoe's life was in turmoil, but she received no assistance from faculty or staff. At home, her parents leaned on her heavily; eventually, something had to give. Her GPA dropped, and Zoe could barely hang on. Her family fought for years to help her brother's long-term recovery, but sadly they lost the battle. Through it all, Zoe felt stigmatized by her brother's addiction; her family was pathologized, and she was embarrassed to reveal to the college what she was going through. Countless phone calls to insurance companies to cover expensive rehab stays, negotiating with police to keep her brother out of jail, and appealing to landlords to allow her brother to keep a roof over his head took up her time and her waning energy but eventually taught her powerful resistance skills. The lessons were hard-won. Although it took time, she learned how to persevere, to ask for what she deserved, and to set boundaries. Of great importance is the compassion she developed for people in the midst of struggle.

Zoe's case does not include personal experiences with racism. However, having responsibility for the care of her brother struggling with addiction led her to feel she was different from other students and to question whether she belonged in college. Zoe's story is relevant in that this type of reflective work can uncover one's experiences with injustice and hardship. The process of going to battle can promote valuable insights. We ask Zoe and other White mentors to reflect on their experiences with exclusion and injustice. What skills have you learned from the adversities in your life? How have your struggles in life shaped your ability to empathize with others? How have you learned to persevere? Do you believe that you can resist with all your might, not win the fight, and still carry on? Engaging in such reflective work may support the Sister Resister's ability to uncover the skills she has and make visible the vulnerabilities of others that emerge in unequal social contexts. Bearing witness to these similarities with people who may seem very different from oneself is fundamental to strong and purposeful mentoring. Mentors and mentees need this relational knowledge and the skills that come with it to become resilient in the face of adversity.

Learning and Applying Resistance to Women's Lives

Race scholar Patricia Hill Collins reminds us that oppression always produces resistance.[12] But not all resistance actions we attempt are prudent, nor are they always in our best interest. In the last chapter, we introduced our theory of resistance, describing it as a developmental competency that refers to the ability to recognize and resist negative social influences and risk behaviors. We talked about the importance of learning to stand up against those who dare to limit who or what you choose to be, and to stand up for what defines the best you can be.[13] The relevance of this theory for White mentors of Black women is twofold. First, mentors can help Black female college students to identify strategies that allow them to resist gender, racial, and class bias in ways that are real, effective, and within their control. Second, we believe that White women benefit immensely from their own personal lessons of resistance. Irrespective of race, there will be times in a woman's life when she must resist the negative forces of social inequity in order to stay safe, psychologically healthy, and true to herself.

Across all class, race, and age groups, women are vulnerable to the use of suboptimal resistance strategies. In an effort to cope with gender subordination, women may think and behave in ways that do not always serve them well and may actually maintain their disempowerment. In an effort to resist feeling unloved and worthless, some women fall victim to the disease to please. In a search to soothe women's inner unrest, some women overeat or undereat and/or rely on alcohol and other drugs.[14]

Women resist in ways that are great and small, individual and collective. The organized Me Too movement of women across the nation rallying against sexual assault and gender-based harassment are powerful testimonies to this resistance. At other times, our efforts are unproductive and completely unsuccessful despite our best attempts. Identifying and opposing the forces of oppression is no easy feat. Poor outcomes—social, physical, and psychological—often follow suboptimally designed, survival-oriented resistance strategies, and they fail to serve women well in the long run.

Our notion of creating a cadre of Sister Resisters rests upon this premise. White women mentors who are willing to interrogate their own personal struggles against oppression—be they gender inequities, class bias, or any other form of societal injustice—can use this knowledge to make connections across social differences with other women engaged in similar battles. Knowledge of the need to effectively resist is inextricably linked to being aware of the forces that Black women resist against.

When White women see Black women's resistance as emerging from the same basic human needs—to be heard, to be respected, to be treated fairly, and to be cared for as human beings—the harmful social biases that negatively impact their identities and constrain women's opportunities become clearer. Standing together with a mentee during a BLM march or sit-in can be life changing for mentors. It is what makes teaching matter. Recognition of this communal experience of resistance—for example, understanding when, why, and who one must stand up for or at times take a stand against—can unite White and Black women as partners in the same struggle.

When Sara was first hired at the university, she was certain that this was her dream job. As a financial aid assistant, Sara thought that as a key decision-maker in her office she'd be able to make a real difference in the lives of her students, particularly those like her who had come to college from low-income backgrounds. And she was right. In no time, students were signing up for appointments with Sara, drawn to her kindness and understanding demeanor. One student after another would share their personal stories of financial distress. As a White woman, Sara also saw how racism was a contributing factor to the barriers Black students were facing as it added to the financial strain they were contending with. Unlike her colleagues, Sara would patiently listen, take notes, and strategize with her clients. The work was emotionally draining, and long after her colleagues had left for the day, Sara would stay behind working the phones, passionately advocating for students in need. She didn't mind working hard for her students, but she resented that her workload was increasing while her male colleagues seemed to look the other way. Exhausted, Sara tried hard to ignore the increasing depression that threatened to overwhelm her. As the only female worker in the office, she felt that she should take care of these students, no matter the cost. She didn't want to complain about the extra work or ask for help as that might make her male colleagues uncomfortable, and she certainly didn't want to let her students down. But she wondered about the unfairness of the situation and how long she could keep this up.

There are many women in the workforce like Sara—women putting in extra unpaid hours while conforming to gendered expectations of caring for others, especially when others are not. Sara is overworked by the demands of the job. She fears offending her male colleagues and is reluctant to push back against gender exploitation. Sara brings many gifts to the table, and they are being devalued and abused. Arguably, she would do well to confront the sexism she has internalized. She could resist feeling that as a woman it is her responsibility to take care of everyone, and she could stand up to her male colleagues, share with them that she feels overworked, and hold them accountable for fulfilling their work responsibilities.

Had Sara engaged in the mentor training that we are proposing, she would participate in a range of self-reflective practices that would lead her to recognize the presence and dynamics of power and oppression in her daily life. This self-awareness, which is central to the work of developing effective resistance, is critical to Sara's empowerment.[15] Situated at the intersection of a privileged and an oppressed identity (e.g., her privileged racial status and her subordinate gender status, not to mention any other invisible intersecting identities), Sara reflects on her experiences of sexism and gender stereotyping. She could use her knowledge of what it feels like to be exploited and devalued as the only woman in the office to resist sexist expectations (her own and others) of her professional behavior. She could use this knowledge to connect with other women, across race, sexuality, and ethnicity, who are doing resistance work. Assembling the building blocks of resistance starts by recognizing that one must identify, name, and ultimately oppose the disempowering forces of discrimination. Mentors who understand sexism and its dynamics of gender and power on a personal level gain a deeper appreciation for how these forces shape the lives of Black female students. They can use that knowledge to connect to and enhance their work with Black women.

Resistance in Action

Margaret's account illustrates the dilemma faced by faculty administrators when they come face to face with questionable decision-making practices within the institution that compound barriers to success.

Margaret is an associate dean and sits on the honor board committee. Today, the committee is discussing the long list of students on the academic warning list. The committee goes from student to student, identifying individual problems that might be preventing students' success. Margaret is feeling increasingly disturbed by the deficit narratives faculty members are using to explain the lagging achievements of the historically marginalized students. She thinks to herself, *Their comments betray their limited knowledge of any alternative culture-based perspectives other than their own.* In her professional position, Margaret has heard many students narrate their exposure to and experiences with race-based bias, microaggressions, and systemic inequities on and off campus. However, when Margaret interjects with alternative ways to think about the difficulties faced by the struggling students of color, faculty defensively interrupt her, minimizing any reference to the toxic racial climate she knows these students are navigating.

Later, Margaret thinks back on the academic meeting, carefully reviewing the racial dynamics that unfolded during the event. As she reread what she had seen and heard, she remembered her colleagues' race-avoidant speech, the way they sugarcoated their words, carefully sidestepping any direct references to race and racism or obliquely referencing matters pertaining to diversity. Margaret thinks that maybe her students are right, that maybe the intellectual, psychological, and social environment for students of color at her college was not conducive to their needs. Annoyed that her colleagues seemed unwilling or unable to comfortably broach topics of race, Margaret feels that she can no longer afford to be silent about the racial inequities her students have brought forward. She knows that naming the racism and speaking up about its impact could be risky. Bringing issues of privilege into the open so that social power can be interrogated by her colleagues may make her unpopular, no longer seen as "one of us"— and who knows what impact it might have on her professional advancement within the institution. Yet Margaret, owning her power, becomes determined to act. She thinks about how she can oppose the barriers that were derailing her students' academic success. She wonders how she can help her students of color develop their own abilities to read, name, and oppose these forces. As a Sister Resister, Margaret sees it as her role to become a responsible decision-maker.

Reflecting on what she should do next, Margaret decides that next time, she'll speak up. She'll expose her colleagues' unexamined assumptions about the race and class identities and backgrounds of their students, and she'll show them how their unrecognized reliance on White norms and expectations exposes their racism and class bias. Margaret will continue to analyze her work with students of color in ways that appreciate the complexity of this work. She will acknowledge all of the visible and invisible identities at play, appreciating the intersectional dynamics that emerge. It is important for Margaret to have support in her resistance; otherwise, she is vulnerable to losing her stride or retreating to more comfortable spaces.

Optimal and effective resistance encourages women's movement in the direction of their dreams. Our voices lifted together is our liberation because we recognize the challenges that exist in our lives to be recognizable among others. Within this framework, the White female mentor uses her self-knowledge and privileged racial status to resist adopting a color-evasive stance. She resists being silent or indifferent in the face of social and institutional bias and discrimination.

Now let's consider Jill. Jill entered her counseling position at the college well prepared to work across cultural differences. Her professional training provided her with the tools she needs to engage in optimal resistance with her student mentees. She is able to collaborate with her student in designing and applying effective strategies of resistance at the university.

Lara is African American, and at twenty-two years old, she is a senior in college. The oldest of five children, she recently learned that her younger sister, a single mother with two small children, has been diagnosed with HIV. Since receiving this news, Lara has been stressed and depressed. While she is worried about her sister's health, she is more uncomfortable about meeting with a White counselor, the only option available this semester in the counseling center. Lara worries that talking about her family and her sister's past sexual history might backfire. She fears that the counselor will believe all of the cultural stereotypes about Black families being disordered and Black women being promiscuous. Fortunately, at her intake, Lara is assigned to a counselor named Jill. The two women speak quietly, exchanging information and checking each other out. Jill considers that Lara may have doubts about working with a White woman. After completing her intake, Jill explains, "This is a very tough road you are on. I would like to walk with you if you will let me. My guess is that we'll probably discuss many difficult and sensitive subjects, and you may decide that you'd prefer to talk with a Black staff member. Might we try this first session, see how you feel afterward, and revisit the question later?" Upon hearing Jill's statement, Lara immediately relaxes. She is grateful that this White woman is brave enough to bring up the issue of race. As her anxiety decreases, Lara glances around Jill's office, noticing the culturally diverse images posted on her walls and the multicultural titles on her bookshelves. There is also a sign on Jill's desk that reads: "Racial oblivion has no home here." Lara takes a deep breath and begins to talk.

Three optimal resistance strategies that intentional mentors can learn from Jill's practice are evident in the preceding case. First, Jill lifts the R word from the shadows: in naming race, Jill extends a message to her Black mentee that says, "I see you. I hear you, and you are not alone. Race is a topic I will not shy away from. I am able and willing to address these issues with you." Second, while Jill offers to help Lara "hold up half the sky," she neither minimizes Lara's concerns nor personalizes the reticence she is experiencing to discuss intimate issues with a White woman. In fact, Jill recognizes that what she has to offer may not be enough. Jill brings an informed knowledge of the cultural histories that have courted the distrust of Blacks and other people of color within mental health settings. Armed with this knowledge, Jill feels empowered to help Lara find someone else (perhaps a woman of color) if necessary, someone who is better able to assist her on her journey. Third, Jill's office sends a message of racial literacy and multicultural appreciation. She is aware of culture and race as critical identities in people's lives, and she continually educates herself by staying abreast of the literature that illuminates these topics. Finally, Jill's signpost on her desk stating that racial oblivion does not reside here communicates to all that she is actively engaged in the work of self-reflection. She is trying to stay racially aware, and she does so by engaging in an inventory of herself as a racial being and by asking hard questions pertaining to racial identity, privilege, and color consciousness. Although the work is complex and often seems never-ending, Jill actively resists retreating into defensiveness. She recognizes that social inequalities are great, but greater still are people working together in meaningful ways to address the solution to our problems. Optimistic about her purpose as an intentional mentor, her lens is not limited by an overblown sense of herself as a racial know-it-all. She still struggles to figure things out. But in understanding that these systems of oppression that we live in are hurting all of us, she knows in her heart that this work someday will set all of us free.

It is empowering to identify ways White female mentors can overcome the social differences they may represent in cross-racial relationships and join with women of color as Sister Resisters. *Sister Resisters* are women who are willing to work together while applying an intersectional lens to resist the people, systems, and institutional arrangements that derail Black students' journeys through higher education. The work of college mentors is made stronger when mentors engage in (1) a willingness to interrogate the meaning of one's race, racial identity, and proximity to racism; (2) a willingness to understand the cultural contexts of the lives of Black female students who attend college; (3) assisting Black women's navigation of the multiple systems of domination that they confront on campus; and (4) working with Black women to design and implement positive resistance strategies in the service of personal, psychological, and academic resilience. This collaborative work between White female mentors and Black female students is essential to an intentional mentoring process that is meaningful and that matters.

CHAPTER 4

Relational Connections and Disconnections

THIS CHAPTER examines Black college women's relationships—with other Black women, with other students and staff on campus, and with White female mentors. We explore the roles that these relationships play in supporting healthy resistance. Here we ask: (1) What dimensions of resistance are supported in Black college women's healthy relationships? (2) What are the tools of resistance that Black college women need to acquire and/or strengthen in order to recognize relationships characterized by value, validation, and veracity? And (3) What critical questions can mentors ask their mentees to assess the quality of their relationships and help them employ effective resistance strategies?

Black Women's Relationships with Other Black Women

Getting through college for young Black women involves engaging in a series of socializing events designed to prepare them for new personal and professional lives. Lessons learned via academic instruction and through social interactions are designed to reinforce new skills that can last a lifetime. We know that many Black students meet other Black students on campus who become lifelong friends.[1] Because of the centrality of relationships in the lives of Black women navigating predominantly White college spaces, we focus our attention in this chapter on what Black students say that they need and desire when making strong relational connections. We tie these desired relational elements to the array of resistance dispositions and skills that we feel are necessary to

Black women's healthy growth and development during their young adult years. In so doing, we explore the relationships that impede strong connections between Black students (and others). These relationships diminish Black women's ability to effectively resist systems of domination. We also highlight what White Sister Resisters can do to tap into their own histories of resistance in order to build and model strong, empowering, and healing relationships with the Black women they work with.

Jackie enters her dorm room, drops her backpack on the floor near her bed, and flings herself face down. Her roommate, Ann Marie, can hear her muffled sobs. She hands a tissue to her friend and waits until she is ready to talk. "He did it again," says Jackie, wiping away tears. "That professor hates me. He chooses the hardest questions, waits, and then calls on *me* to answer in front of the class. 'What's the matter, Miss Washington?,' he says in that condescending tone. 'You don't know this, even though we've gone over this equation many times in class? Do we all have to do it again because *you* just can't seem to get it? How did you get into this program anyway?'" The two young women sit in silence for a moment. "It was so embarrassing," Jackie says, sniffling. "Everyone was staring at me. Even I started to wonder why I'm in that program."

"Come on, girl," says Ann Marie. "You know you're exactly where you should be. That man has done this before, and he's probably going to do it again. That's his problem, not yours. And I heard he does this every year with all the Black students who take his class. He knows if you don't pass his class, you don't move on in the program, and that's exactly what he wants. We ain't giving him the satisfaction. You came here to do premed, and you are going to medical school. You've come too far to quit now. We need you, Dr. Washington! Come on—let's figure out what you gotta do to get through this class."

Scenes like this, with Black students offering each other support in response to a moment of doubt and uncertainty, recur frequently in campus spaces and is an important form of peer mentoring.[2] Black women turn to their friends for solace, particularly when racially charged situations arise that make students feel trapped and frustrated. In responding to her friend's distress, Ann Marie doesn't downplay the role of racial bias in the instructor's interactions. She makes connections to past events and points out that he routinely disparages Black students in his class, perhaps purposefully pushing them out of the program. Jackie feels affirmed when talking about these troubles with her roommate. They are both aware of institutional racism and the "push-out" behaviors (suspensions, disciplinary hearings, academic probation, and expulsion) that disproportionately target Black students routinely in schools and colleges.[3] Together they establish the criteria needed (that this is a behavioral and attitudinal pattern of bias) and they give themselves permission to name the phenomenon they believe is unfolding. In doing so, rather than being paralyzed by the acknowledgment of racial bias, Ann Marie and Jackie are emboldened to act. They know what they are fighting against. They understand what's at stake. They respect themselves and the educational journey they have committed to. And they believe in their power to stand strong in the face of those who would diminish their dreams. In this relatively brief moment of relational connection, two Black women, sister friends, replenish in each other their "warrior spirits." They remind each other that the battle for racial justice in health care doesn't stop in the classroom. The fight continues; it matters, and with the right focus, skills, and determination, they've got what it takes to win.

Researchers have long argued the centrality of relationships in the lives of women and have shown the many ways that women come to articulate who they are, what they want in life, and what they value through their friendships with other women.[4] Some of these relationships are long term and all encompassing; others are short term and instrumental. Martínez-Alemán puts it well when she writes that women's friendships in college are relationships in which women can experience learning that is "purposeful, practical, and productive."[5]

On and off campus, higher education institutions support spaces where cross-racial friendships may emerge—sports teams, university-sanctioned clubs, residential housing, and the like.[6] Nonetheless, researchers find that, similar to their White counterparts, many Black female students prefer to socialize primarily with students who are similar to themselves.[7] This is particularly true among Black students who are strongly race-identified. Friendships in college tend to be based on mutual interests or on the emotional or psychological needs that women may possess. Major life events unfold in college, such as dealing with the feelings associated with living away from home for the first time. Resolving roommate conflicts, negotiating romantic relationships, handling academic achievement, or coping with academic distress are situations typically shared with the new friends made in college. Friends learn to rely on and trust each other, which can minimize loneliness and despair. Whether motivated by feelings of racial isolation, marginalization, racial objectification, or tokenism, Black students tend to seek comfort with other Black students who are facing similar challenges that are racially charged.

Finding a community of students who appreciate their racialized and gendered experiences and with whom they feel they can create authentic and respectful peer relationships becomes, in these environments, a relational priority. Black women seek out other women who share a sense of collectivism and commitment to the well-being and empowerment of their group.[8] They want to find and create spaces where Black students feel their racial and gender identities will be affirmed. Black student organizations, Black student unions (BSUs), Black sororities, and similar organizations often fulfill these needs.[9] An added advantage can be that the relationships created within these groups can create "spaces of resistance and sustainability against institutional norms that oppress and marginalize Black women."[10]

Campus friendships expose Black women to ethnically diverse, gender diverse, and regionally diverse Black women. These connections can be quite helpful to women as they seek academic support, find opportunities for career advancement, and even navigate sorority life. The creation of long-term, meaningful relationships and of strong social networks are especially important when Black women confront bias, microaggressions, and other forms of mistreatment in and outside of the classroom. For these reasons, we often worry when we find a Black student feeling isolated and alone, lacking a supportive network of friends—especially other Black women or other women of color. Students need places to connect and decompress. Affinity groups such as BSUs and Black sororities create spaces where, Walton and Oyewuwo-Gassikia say, Black women participate in acts of "sisterhood, self-love and positive affirmation."[11] It's in these spaces that Black women can revel in the fact that *we got through this together* and *there ain't no stopping us now.*

Intraracial, Interethnic, and Class-Related Conflict

For years I (Janie) taught a course that examined Black music and other cultural productions created in the 1960s and 1970s, from the Black liberation movements (the civil rights and Black power movements) through disco to the advent of hip-hop. In one semester I had a self-identified Black nerd in my class—a "blerd," she called herself. She was a gifted writer who enjoyed reading anime and comic books and writing Black sci-fi and fantasy. The other women in class found her introverted, awkward, and lacking social skills. But they also were the first to defend her when students outside of class dared to tease her or question her racial identity. "What?!" they'd say, "There can't be Black nerds?!" This young sister had a keen sense of who she was and the kind of writer she wanted to become. She knew what piqued her interest and set her mind and heart free. Some writers, observing the increasing influence of Afrofuturism, technoculture, and Black science fiction today, argue that we are witnessing "an emergent political insurgency similar to the Black Arts Movement that unfolded fifty years ago." Journalist Adam Bradley believes that Black artists "are increasingly drawn to speculative fiction and fantasy, horror and weird fiction as a necessary respite from the unrelenting pressure of combating White supremacy, and as a creative resource for addressing present-day challenges."[12] Blerds like my student challenge stereotypes and redefine Black identity. They create spaces for Black imagination and innovation, proclaiming to the world that they too are Black, proud, and welcomed members of the tribe.

Naturally, from time to time, there may be issues that come up between Black women and within Black women's groups that can instigate interpersonal conflicts and create barriers to positive identity development and community building. Not everyone reads their racial or gendered reality in the same way. Differences—say, in sexuality, religion, or politics—can emerge between Black women based on where they are in their levels of race and gender consciousness. This includes how they feel about their race and gender identities at a personal level and the degree to which they feel a sense of belonging to others who they regard as culturally similar. Given the wide range of diversity within the population of students of African descent, even the term *culture* can be loaded and misunderstood. Our students (or their families) hail from nations on the African continent, from the Caribbean islands, and from Central and South America—all locations with their own racial histories and heritage. For Black immigrant women, or students maintaining strong connections to their national and ethnocultural customs and traditions, how one thinks about the prevalence of racism and the decisions about when and whether one confronts race as an issue may differ significantly. For biracial and multiracial women, how they self-categorize, integrate, and affirm their identities can be complex and intensely personal. Identifying as queer or trans reshapes racial identity, friendships, and who you might consider an ally. The work undertaken by Black students to negotiate their multiple identities—that is, what they put emphasis on, what they see as more or less salient and why, what they explore and celebrate—are all self-defining elements of identity construction, and they play out in as many iterations as there are Black women.

Priscilla was born outside the United States. The intermittent conflict in her country drove Priscilla and her mother to escape from the Democratic Republic of the Congo (DRC) a few years ago, when she was in high school. It was a long, dangerous, and politically complicated journey out of the DRC, which they managed even as they were denied documentation that would protect them in the United States. Now Priscilla's immigration status may be in question. With no way to access federal financial aid, Priscilla paid for her first two years of school out of pocket with money she had earned working on the Holiday Inn's housekeeping staff for two full years before her first year in college. Now she's out of money, and her lack of proper documentation has adversely impacted her ability to secure the college's financial aid or any of the other available loans other students can apply for to pay their tuition bills. Moreover, Priscilla just learned that she may be barred from applying to the internship she needs to finish her degree requirements, and until she can legalize her immigration status, there is a good chance that she will be blocked from future employment opportunities.

Undocumented Black students face legal uncertainties and a host of limitations that other Black students may not face. Often, undocumented students are embarrassed about their status. They feel stigmatized and marginalized, with the fear of being found out and possibly deported always hanging over their heads. Students like Priscilla may be members of the Black student population, anxious and frightened while at the same time trying to balance their academic studies and adjust to American culture, the college system, and campus life.

Unfortunately, Black people are not immune to mean-spirited, discriminatory attitudes and petty actions inflicted against Black people from geographically foreign lands. Accents and difficulties expressing oneself in English as a second (or third or fourth) language can be ridiculed, regarded with contempt, and deemed inferior.[13] Groups can be culturally snobbish and condescending toward others, despite all sharing skin color similarities. We have heard Caribbean Blacks say that relatives warn them to stay away from Black Americans. Black Americans, they have been told, are lazy, don't value education, and will only drag you down. We have seen Black foreign-born students struggle to reconcile the messages they had received from family about academic achievement and hard work being enough to overcome discrimination. The hard cold truth is that racism is real. Industry, ambition, and achievement, although critical to resistance, are not enough to erase the pernicious effects of racism.

Intraracial interpersonal conflicts can also center on social class differences students bring onto campus. College might be the first time students are exposed to other students who have grown up in very different social and economic backgrounds. Every year, we have heard stories of some students vacating residence halls, heading down to Florida, Cancun, or some warm Caribbean island for spring break, while others remain stuck on campus, financially unable to make the trip. Tuition, for some students, is easily covered by family; others must work two and three jobs to pay the bills. Hidden costs of college—student fees, textbooks, lunches and dinners not covered by the meal plan—can be more than a minor inconvenience. Being the one who does not have enough money when surrounded by others who seem to have more than what is fair can be painfully tough. And that pain can be exacerbated when the student looks like you.

"She thinks she's better than me because her family has money," whined Adrienne. "And I heard she and her stuck-up friends look down on the girls like me, the girls who can't afford the clothes and the trips and all that. When we party and get a little loud, you know, having the only kind of fun we can enjoy without going broke, I heard they call us ghetto and stuff. Like being broke makes you less than, you know what I mean?"

Another third rail of intraracial conflict is the persistent problem of colorism—the problem that just won't go away.[14] *Colorism* is best described as internalized bias and favor for a distinct set of phenotypic characteristics that include lighter skin, Eurocentric facial features (e.g., thin nose and thin lips), and "good" hair texture (e.g., hair that is long or straight or wavy, rather than tightly coiled and/or kinky). Skin color operates as a form of social capital; it reflects a form of social power and unearned privilege that both produces and reproduces inequality. This privilege translates into educational attainment, upwardly mobile social networks, greater income opportunities, and access to higher-earning dating partners and potential spouses. Often, colorist attitudes take root in the family and in the early years of young women's lives. As they grow up, exposure to visual and print media heavily perpetuate colorist notions, particularly through the entertainment, beauty, fashion, and advertising industries. Images are slowly changing here and there, but few women can escape the destructive undertones of the "light is right" message and its effect on Black women's self-esteem.

Years ago, we interviewed high school and college students about their experiences with colorism.[15] As Black women find themselves dating in their college years, colorist preferences may influence the attitudes of their romantic partners regarding their skin color and hair. For example, a young undergraduate student in one of our classes once shared that when she reached adolescence, she was told that she was too dark to be considered cute by guys. We have heard stories of queer, light-skinned Black students feeling color-fetishized in queer circles and, in intimate relations, feeling objectified by White women curious about their hair.

Being grounded within healthy relationships for Black women is not simply a nice added feature of the college experience: it is a requirement—indeed, we would argue, a lifeline. For some Black women, the building blocks of resistance start with the acquisition of knowledge gained from other Black women in affinity groups. This is where stereotypes are refuted and the diversity of Black identities are affirmed.

Due to the pervasive nature of racism in society and in higher education, Black college women are too often targets of self-annihilating racist acts. Racist discourses do not skip over Black college women. They become internalized until they are confronted and replaced within a resistance frame. Stereotypic discourses about Black people cause challenges for Black college women forming relationships with other Black peers across ethnic, class, and other dimensions of difference. Through film, cartoons, and media, Black women are exposed to the same demeaning messages about Black people that exist in the broader society. Images of Black women as loud, large bodied, sassy, aggressive, and overly religious erode relationship formation among people who are racially similar but are different across other identities.[16] These negative images of Black people in general and Black women in particular can shape a student's reticence to identify with Black affinity groups.

Black Women's and White Mentors' Relationships and Resistance

Cross-racial interactions in college potentially promote a host of positive outcomes. The benefits of these interactions to Black students are plentiful. For example, they learn valuable information from members of groups that differ from one's own. They develop pride, identity, and community within the college setting. They gain exposure to differing political ideologies and they develop an interest in and understanding of issues affecting others in their age group.[17] In predominantly White institutions, Black students frequently socialize across race. They live and eat together with White students, they work with them in study groups, and sometimes they date interracially. Most of the time, these interactions function fairly well. However, students have shared with us, and with other researchers, a wide range of interpersonal tensions with their White female counterparts that surface in college classrooms, in residence halls, and in other social settings. We draw attention to these troublesome situations not to dwell on what can go wrong in cross-racial interactions but to illuminate the power of interracial relationships between women to educate, support, and strengthen both groups involved. There is a role for White women, particularly Sister Resisters, to play in assisting and reinforcing the healthy resistance strategies undertaken by Black female students. To do so requires that we identify what goes wrong in interracial communications as the first step to understanding how these relationships can be constructed differently for success.

We begin with what researchers have found to impede cross-racial connections. A primary annoyance shared by Black women in predominantly White institutions relates to racial misperceptions and unexamined assumptions about them that can lead to troublesome interactions, particularly with their White female counterparts. Black women are quite articulate in explaining what's at the root of these misunderstandings. "They really don't know us," says Rayna. "Most of them went to all-White schools. Living with me is the closest they've ever been to racial diversity." Rayna and most other Black students know that depending on where a college is located, or on the population of students drawn to and enrolled in a particular institution, majority students often enter college with very few prior close encounters with Black students and their families. Across the United States, White students often grow up in predominantly White schools and communities with few students who are racially different. If there were Black students attending their elementary and high schools, those "minority" students may have been "one ofs" (that is, one of the only Black kids in advanced chemistry or another AP class). Students of color in majority schools are often clustered in lower-level academic programs, where they have minimal contact with the majority of White students on campus.[18] For White students socialized in these types of racially segregated educational settings, being around other White students was familiar and comfortable. Being around racially different students was unusual and strange. In the absence of direct, firsthand experiences with students whose social backgrounds and cultural practices are largely unknown, that lack of knowledge is often replaced with erroneous and even dangerous stereotypes.

Black students complain that White students base what they think they know about Black people on images gleaned from popular culture, TV, and film. In their minds, Black women are irreverent, loud, and demonstrative. They are assumed to reside in or near low-income, violent, and dangerous neighborhoods with questionable values and little to offer. Being Black in a dormitory setting can be particularly treacherous. In residence halls, where students are exposed to one another's intimate daily grooming rituals, Black women say that they find the imposition of European standards of beauty relentless and inescapable. They complain, for example, that White women have an endless fascination with Black hair. How Black women wash, dry, moisturize, straighten, curl, braid, lock, twist, comb, pick, and otherwise groom their hair can be confusing if that is not what you observed growing up. It's when White women impose their sense of what Black women should be doing with their hair that all hell breaks loose. The imposition of the White beauty ideal (e.g., hair styles expected to be long or straight like those of White women) is what makes Black women feel they've been victimized by a feminized form of racism. Rather than having their attractiveness affirmed, they are being told that what is considered attractive should be acceptable to the White establishment. Like colorism, this objectifying of Black women's bodies (hair) is yet another form of upholding patriarchy. Only this time it involves women holding other women to standards created by and mostly for the pleasures and preferences of men.

In many spaces within predominantly White institutions, Black women feel that their behavior is scrutinized in ways that are different from other students in the dormitory. When they congregate together, Black women feel they are being watched, assessed, and judged by their White female counterparts. It's a daily struggle for Black women to hold onto their identities and racial preferences. They feel exposed and disapproved of for their dress, their hair and makeup, and their language usage. Some feel compelled to keep quiet about these concerns in order to keep the peace. They find themselves walking on eggshells in hopes of avoiding a slip up or an unpleasant encounter in the dorm or with a roommate. As a result, Black female students report that they prefer to hang out with groups who have other marginalized identities—lesbian and gender nonconforming, other women of color, religious minorities, or first-generation students—populations who are themselves stigmatized or feel different on campus.

Obviously, not all cross-racial interactions are fraught with tension, but there is much in the research to suggest that Black female students in predominantly White colleges often feel misunderstood by their White female (and male) peers. It is clear that such perceptions and unpleasant interactions can lead to psychological stress, anger, cynicism, and relational detachment. In one of the focus groups we facilitated, a participant described that when on campus, she often feels like she is swimming through a sea of judgmental White girls. Her attitude supports the view of many students of color that college just doesn't feel like a safe place to be.

Interracial tensions in residence halls can emerge from relatively innocent interpersonal conflicts, as well as from more overt misunderstandings and assaultive microaggressions. Blatant racial hostilities and hate crimes on college campuses are on the rise. Race-themed parties continue to make the national news. Black female students say that in dorm halls, when more than two Black students assemble together, they are perceived as threatening and suspicious. When their guests are Black or Brown and male, the escalating fear level among the White dormitory residents can lead to heightened tension and unwarranted calls to campus security.

Eunice and Alison are the two RAs assigned to the second floor in their college's coed dormitory. This semester has been particularly challenging. Students have complained bitterly about minor, though unrelenting interactions involving a group of White students who, according to the Black students, are being disrespectful and intentionally annoying. The Black students want the White students held accountable. Alison, who is White, is sympathetic to the Black students, but she feels woefully ill-equipped to intervene. She says to Eunice, "I know those girls. They're in my biology class. I don't know what to say to them, and I really don't want to get involved. Besides, it will stop soon. They're just blowing off steam." But the behavior doesn't stop, even after Eunice talks to the offending students in an attempt to diffuse the situation. Ten weeks into the semester, neither group is backing down. Eunice hesitates to report the White girls to the head of Residence Life. In the past, she has found that when Black RAs speak up about race, their perspectives are often dismissed or their suggestions are undermined by those in authority. Brushing things off, Alison suggests, "Just forget about it." But it's not that easy for Eunice. As the Black RA, she is the person who everyone expects to resolve all of the racial conflicts that erupt in the dormitories. She is expected to carry the emotional burden of the students' race-based anger, distrust, and frustration. Eunice is exhausted by it all, and even though she desperately needs the financial aid that comes with the job, she doubts if she'll sign up again for another RA position.

Differences in the social capital students bring with them to campus have their own way of creating tensions that can undermine relationships between women. How college students experience their downtime is highly dependent on their financial situation. Drinking and partying on weekends at local bars and restaurants versus spending one's free time on campus is often tied to what students can afford. Similarly, being able to afford necessary textbooks or computer software for class or being able to accept an unpaid internship or enroll in a study abroad program depends on extra income that many students, Black and White, just do not have. For them, the college years are about balancing paid employment with academic demands. Economic and racial disparities are often exacerbated on predominantly White college campuses. We may want to believe that colleges are settings in which close friendships are made and where students with less privilege acquire access to the professional success networks commonly reserved for members of more privileged groups, but often this is not the case. Although certainly not the primary purpose for Black students' friendships with White students, Black students could benefit from the networking power that White students may possess to advance professionally and financially. But that can only happen when students feel invested and safe enough to do the work of connecting across their differences.

Reconstituting Cross-Racial Relationships that Support Healthy Resistance

Despite the many ways in which cross-racial relationships between Black and White women can go awry, it is also true that these relationships can and do flourish in college classrooms and across campuses. Young women come together and bridge their differences when they have shared experiences, when they see similarities in their interests, and when personality characteristics such as openness, caring, empathy, and honesty are held in common.

In earlier chapters, we introduced the requisite knowledge, attitudes, and dispositional traits of mentors who we feel are best suited to function as Sister Resisters in their work with Black female students. Here we speak to the elements in cross-racial pairings between White mentors (who are most often female) and Black female students that create open, authentic, and respectful mentoring relationships. Racial differences are only one of the many social identities that could be in tension in a mentoring relationship. Age differences, differences in regional and social backgrounds, linguistic differences, and even disciplinary differences can and do at times matter. Similarly, personalities may clash, and no matter what they do, sometimes mentors and mentees simply do not click. Setting aside the variances of human factors that can be neither controlled nor predicted in the process of forming or sustaining a relationship, we argue that the relationships that Sister Resisters need to establish with their Black mentees have a number of unique and specific characteristics. These characteristics include exercising the ability to challenge gendered racial stereotypes, embracing cultural humility, knowing and interrogating one's own racial history, and engaging in an ongoing process of developing one's racial literacy.

There's this one table in the Student Life cafeteria that catches the eyes and ears of people passing through. There's usually a small group of Black students crowded around a table or two, grabbing a quick meal or drink between classes. Every few minutes a burst of laughter will erupt and a loud cackle, uproarious giggles, a hard slap on the tabletop, and an "Oooh girl—you're so right!!" will lift the volume of the whole room. Some of the other students will turn and stare, but the Black students never seem to care. They thoroughly enjoy their time together, telling stories, giving advice, trading suggestions about everything from passing exams to how to talk with financial aid officers. Black women know how to crack each other up, and Lord knows they enjoy doing so. If you come on a Monday, you'll see Professor London at the table too. An English professor, she is an honorary Sista friend. She got that designation one year during orientation, when a few students overheard her make a witty quip that caused everyone to burst out laughing. It turned out that her course on Shakespeare, while demanding, was filled with such humor, and soon hers became the go-to class for Black women fulfilling their humanities requirements. Unlike the other White students and faculty who seemed to steer clear of the table with the "loud Black girls," Professor London loved their energy and decided that's where she'd prefer to be. Since then, she's been there every Monday, having a good time with the rest of them.

Aided by folktales, proverbs, ritualized insults (playing the dozens), signifyin', and loud-talking, Black folks across generations have engaged in a long history of some serious joke-making. Arising from the unrelenting instances of racial injustice since our involuntary arrival on these shores, and the dangerous racial situations that we have had to endure, we have, as they say, used our laughter to keep from crying. Black folks' humor, a tool often used by those in power to demean and dismiss African people, can, "through inversion on the part of the oppressed, become a weapon of liberation."[19] Did Professor London know this? Perhaps, or maybe not. What is evident is her ability to use humor to connect with others. Finding ways to connect with student mentees is an important skill for mentors to acquire.

We have much to learn from what Black female students say they are looking for in their friendships and other associations, largely (although not exclusively) with other Black women. They seek out people they can talk to about their racial reality. They want individuals who will not shy away from race talk—women who are willing and able to read the environment for racial and gender bias and to share a willingness to truthfully name and call out racially charged bias when they see it. Black women know the benefits of sisterhood, particularly in settings where they are the minority, and they appreciate the gold mine of cultural knowledge and emotional dispositions Black women possess, as well as the repertoire of effective resistance strategies they have honed over the years. We argue that Sister Resisters would do well to study and emulate the Black women's relationships described earlier in this chapter. There is much to listen to and learn from these women who have figured out how to trust, love, and care for each other, even in environments where they themselves may feel uncared for. Most importantly, they have figured out how to support one another's resistance against the powerful negative reinforcement of oppressive tropes and how to recover from their onslaught in all forms.

Cassidy's story is a reflection of the pivotal role of campus life in shaping Black students' identity development. Student relationships within campus organizations can support Black students' resistance to harmful discourses and can assist in building community across differences. Similarly, office hours, where faculty make space for and in fact encourage people to visit, collectively support students' friendships in an intellectual space. Conversations may occur that might not happen elsewhere. It is a space where the mentor can witness the power of friendships among women of color and the creation of resistance culture.

Cassidy is a second-year student attending a large research institution in the Northeast. Her mother is Jewish and her father is Latino and from the Dominican Republic. She jokingly says her dad looks like the twin of Boston Red Sox legend David Ortiz. Throughout her life, Cassidy has identified as Jewish and Latina. She speaks Hebrew and Spanish and has traveled internationally. Cassidy is phenotypically similar to other Black college students. They read her as Black, as have others, locally and abroad. "All of these people," Cassidy complains, "keep mistaking me for someone who I clearly am not." Cassidy does not perceive a need to connect with Black students on campus nor to identify with Black people in general. As part of a sociology class assignment, Dr. Jacobs, who is also Jewish, asked her students to enter a space on campus they had not previously attended and discuss why they had not done so. Cassidy was unsure what to do for the assignment and spoke to Dr. Jacobs for guidance. The professor recommended that Cassidy attend a Black Diasporic affinity group, and much to Cassidy's surprise, there she connected with other Black students similar to herself, multiracial and members of religious minorities. Once she made the connection, Cassidy's attendance continued well beyond submission of the assignment.

The Black student affinity group that Cassidy attended allowed her to become aware of her own racial isolation as she listened to and spoke with others. This process of watching others take risks to divulge personal information cultivated trust and modeled for Cassidy different yet affirming ways of being Black.

Bearing witness to the oppression that Black people have been subjected to and having the ability to see and name this oppression define the primary skills of resistance. It is distressing to hear people's struggles with racial inequity, and even more distressing to share your own. Naming this oppression in healthy relational spaces becomes possible when students, across ethnic and linguistic diversity, recognize ways of speaking about race that they all understand to explain, interpret, and manage oppression.

Cassidy's affinity group created a safe environment for her to examine the racism around her, explore her own Black racial identity, and interrogate the ways in which she has unwittingly internalized racialized discourses. By speaking and listening to her new friends, she began to confront and gradually unlearn the attitudes that failed to support her Black identity as a multiracial person. For example, in Cassidy's family of origin, there was an absence of talk or, better yet, concealed silence about race, racism, and skin color. By awakening to the reality of how deeply race had shaped her identity, Cassidy was able to reflect upon the routine experiences with microaggressions that both she and other darker-skinned members of her family had frequently endured.

Within healthy relationships, students examine the beliefs about Blackness that they may have unknowingly internalized in society from parents, teachers, clergy, and the media. By becoming informed about the messages they received from their homes and communities, students can identify and critique the racialized discourses used to pit Black people against one another. When Cassidy was growing up, she heard a host of erroneous messages, like those suggesting that all Black students were low income and first generation, as well as dangerously hurtful messages suggesting that lighter skin is more attractive and more desirable than darker shades. These tropes contributed to Cassidy's disavowal of her Black heritage. They fostered low regard for her beautiful brown skin, and they led her to distance herself from Black people, who she regarded as unattractive and inferior. Exposure to diversity among racially similar people afforded her the opportunity to reflect upon how damaging discourses are transmitted within families.

Listening to her new friends gave her the tools to resist, refute, and replace these discourses over time.

One of the positive outcomes for Black college women when making strong connections with a diverse group of Black college peers is that strong, culturally specific, social and psychological resistance frameworks can be built. Here we are talking about the relational implications of antiracist work. Learning to see and name divisive caste and color divisions and learning how to resist internalizing these negative self-images is a particular benefit of healthy intraracial relationships. When students like Cassidy apply their critical consciousness and uncover information about their racial identity that had been previously hidden or obscured by family members and loved ones, their worldviews may be shaken, followed sometimes by emotional distress. *Cognitive dissonance*, the psychological stress of having to hold contradictory ideas, values, and beliefs, can use up much-needed psychic energy.[20] Dealing with these complicated thoughts all alone can be especially taxing. But these moments also have the ability to transform the oppressive attitudes that hold young women and could foster empowerment and liberation.[21] Cassidy was very fortunate to have Dr. Jacobs in her life. Dr. Jacobs exhibited many of the characteristics associated with being a Sister Resister. She created an environment of trust and validation. She listened attentively to Cassidy's conflict, and she helped her to identify a safe space on campus to do the identity work that she needed to do. As a result, Cassidy became awake to unsettling memories of being devalued and discounted. Fortunately, confronting and sharing these memories with others who could relate was transformational to Cassidy's journey toward becoming comfortable with who she is. Through discussions with others, Cassidy came to see herself as belonging to an affirming community that she had earlier dismissed and previously regarded as unimportant.

Seeing and naming oppression is foundational to opposing and replacing various forms of discrimination. Students can learn ways beyond knowing and learn how to make a difference that is linked to purpose and social justice. As a function of actively participating in the affinity group, Cassidy continued to share her experiences with Dr. Jacobs. During one conversation, Dr. Jacobs told Cassidy that she had recommended her attendance at the Black Diasporic group because she herself had disavowed her Jewish identity during her college years. A Jewish affinity group was transformational for her, and in that space she was able to confront the discourses about people of the Jewish faith that led her to hide her history, culture, and language.

The relationships that Sister Resisters build with Black women are the spaces in which both women, concurrently, learn to see and name the oppressions that influence their lives. Mentees, either individually or together with a strong and intentional Sister Resister, can codesign effective strategies to mitigate the effect of such oppressions. It is in these relationships that women dialogue and exchange ideas. They discuss issues at the experiential level, creating space for the raw emotions that emerge when women challenge the oppression and privilege associated with their class, gender, sexuality, and other identities. They learn ways of being that contribute to positive self-development, affirm one's identity (personal and reference group), and keep Black women on the path to social and academic success. And, as we saw earlier with Cassidy, sometimes these relationships serve to help Black women unlearn problematic attitudes and behaviors in order to move forward. White women, too, at the same time, can grow in their ability to resist sexism, patriarchy, and White supremacy. These lessons gleaned from the lived experiences of Black women have the ability to fortify White women. Tapping the power of relational connection, Sister Resisters nurture change and inspire growth, individually and together.

Value, Validation, and Veracity

Throughout this book, we have spoken truth to power—that racism and other forms of oppression are invalidating. The forces of injustice maintain that people, by virtue of the color, shape, and arc of their bodies, have different levels of importance and value. These messages inform policies, practices, and priorities and become representations of truth. Resistance is also a force. It is more powerful than the injustice it denounces because it is seeded in love. Sister Resister mentoring relationships pivot the gaze and declare to oppression that it has not won. That it does not represent the truth. Humans are more similar than they are different, and together we harness the might of the universe through our relational connections with one another. People can be changed at depth and for the better. In this moment and at this time, we reclaim and recast value, validation, and veracity as the soul of optimal resistance.

In general, *value* refers to the importance, worth, or usefulness of something or someone. Value is witnessed through prioritization. In valuing their relationship, a mentor and mentee grasp the significance of their bond, knowing that it matters, both in the short and long term. Because the relationship matters, time is devoted to and set aside for communing and conversing. Meetings that are cancelled are rescheduled at their earliest convenience because the connection that has been made is deemed valuable. The necessity of checking in, hearing from the mentee, and having the mentee on the mentor's radar sends a message: I am yours, and you are mine. While healthy boundaries are established, the mentor knows what is going on with her mentee and can answer the question, "What help does my mentee need?" Problems are noticed in a timely manner, and when needed, plans of action are promptly set in motion. Difficult topics are not silenced.

Value is seen in the mentee's strong belief that her mentor can say her name, knows where she comes from, and knows who her people are. The mentor is familiar with her mentee's coming to college story, knows what her major is, and is genuinely interested in her mentee's progress. Their journey together is valued, and the mentee feels cared for and trusts that her mentor is there to support her identity development and will help her feel like she belongs at college. Sister Resisters ask themselves, Am I meeting the needs of my mentee? In supporting her journey, am I doing my own work and sharing what I know about how to resist in healthy and effective ways?

Validation speaks to the act of "accepting someone else's internal experience as valid and understandable."[22] Truthful, fearless, and honest talk about racism with one's mentee can be a hard conversation for mentors to elicit and even harder for them to hear. But a Sister Resister must be emotionally available, nonjudgmental, and genuinely interested, with the capacity to honor her mentees' words. She does not minimize her mentee's feelings, ignore her life experiences, or deflect—by changing the subject or by hiding behind humor to flee from distressing conversations about injustice. Mentors are in touch with what matters to them in their relationship. They are aware of what is needed for both women to prosper as Sister Resisters. What needs to be said is said. The relational connection is cherished. And should a serious problem arise between the two women, there is clarity about when disconnecting may be best for the relationship.

Although agreement is not required for harmony to exist, there must be a shared respect for differences in opinion that surface and a brave space for those differences to be openly expressed. In cross-racial relationships that matter, Black students need to trust that they are being listened to. The mentee's triumphs, including great grades, awards, presentations, grants, and study abroad opportunities, are celebrated. And all of this work is possible, even in the midst of the intense busyness of university life. The mentor provides thoughtful advice about her mentee's academic and professional plans and will identify the structures and mechanisms of racism and sexism that the mentee will most likely confront during her college years and beyond.

Both women need to feel validated in this struggle to confront oppression; otherwise, the experience can feel isolating, overwhelming, and simply too hard to endure. Sister Resisters ask themselves, Am I able to detect where my mentee experiences this college as invalidating? Where on this campus do students receive the message that their narratives, histories, and experiences are less relevant? Am I doing the best that I can to understand the psychological effects of living with racism on my college campus? Do I fully appreciate how racism can interfere with my mentee's academic performance and damage her physical and mental health?

Veracity speaks to the discernments of truth, authenticity, and legitimacy. It refers to the quality of being true, honest, and accurate. Within strong and intentional mentoring relationships, Sister Resisters can support their Black mentees in developing the social, moral, and emotional capacities that allow mentees to make sense of and successfully navigate the inequities of social injustices. Being truthful is central to this project. Systemic oppression is a reality. Those who dare to call it out are not promoting victimhood, nor are they denying the social progress that we as a nation have made. Being honest about where we are as a country and the work that lies in front of us as a people is as important as being truthful in how we speak, listen, and interact within cross-racial relationships.

Discernment skills allow Black mentees to trust that their relationships with their mentors are testaments to what they believe their relationships to be. Sister Resisters are guided by commitment, a strong moral stance against the tyranny of oppression, and a conviction that wrong in all its forms must be stared down and called out. These acts of habitual honesty create a courageous and caring context to address and work through gendered racial or cultural conflicts that arise in the mentoring relationship. Sister Resisters ask themselves, Am I creating a safe and brave space for my mentee to talk and be heard? What is the evidence of my speaking truth to power?

The capacity to identify and stay true to one's thoughts and emotions is core to discerning healthy relationships, particularly when a woman's values run contrary to gendered and/or cultural expectations. Healthy relationships make life worth living. This preeminent knowledge is vital for Black college women to secure within their resistance tool kits. But the ability to discern actions, affects, and thoughts that are linked to healthy relationships from those that are mired in toxicity is an essential developmental competency. These skills have to be reinforced; they are vulnerable to being lost by young women who are too often socialized to be selfless and silent about their needs.

Mentors have their mentees on their minds. Emma is an African American nursing student. She is tired of being mistaken as the maintenance staff at the hospital where she interns, despite wearing an ID with her name and scrubs that match those of her White peers. She is weary of the disrespect and is thinking of dropping out of the nursing program. *Veracity* allows the Sister Resister to alert her mentee to the danger that she sees coming and to say, "I think leaving now is not in your best interest. You will face racism wherever you go. Let's talk about how you can stay at the hospital and what we can do to change this situation."

Corine is a non-traditional-age undergraduate who recently returned to college to finish her degree. Her education was previously interrupted when she had to take time off and assist her parents in keeping their small neighborhood restaurant afloat. On weekends, Corine still returns home to help out. Between the commute and the long hours, sometimes Corine's academic work takes a back seat. *Validation* emboldens the Sister Resister to gently broach this dilemma: "Some of your faculty do not understand or agree with your decision to rush home, leave campus, and miss deadlines to work in your family's restaurant. I respect your devotion to your family and your responsibilities as the eldest daughter, but your frequent departures have negatively impacted your grades. Let's see what we can do to better manage your schedule."

Vyn was really excited to be accepted to her college. She arrived on the college campus from a large, underserved city high school and quickly fit in. Although eager and studious, Vyn is finding that in her upper-level classes, her analytic writing is becoming a problem. Her mentor has seen her assignments and observes that she needs considerable help. *Value* enables the Sister Resister to gently confront Vyn and say: "I care about you and I care about what happens to you. You belong here; you have worked hard to get into this program. Secure some assistance from the writing center. An editor will help you to improve your writing, particularly since graduate school is on your radar. I will help you identify the assistance you need."

In the following example, Mindy, with the help of her mentor, Meg, demonstrates decision-making that reflects value, validation, and veracity in her practice of resistance and illustrates how resistance can be elevated by a thoughtful and caring mentor.

Mindy is a second-year college student. She identifies as bisexual and has been dating Ronny for a short time. She would like to begin a sexual relationship with Ronny. She also wants to get tested for a sexually transmitted infection (STI) and wants Ronny to get tested as well and to make condom use a regular part of their sexual life. Mindy shares her thoughts with Ronny, who tells her that he is not going to get tested and that other women don't pressure him like Mindy is doing. He does not like the feel of condoms and won't use them. Mindy ends the relationship with Ronny. Although she initially thought she had made the right choice, she misses Ronny and doubts her decision. Feeling distressed, Mindy contacts Meg, a mentor assigned to her during her first year with whom she meets regularly. Meg is a nurse and works on campus in Student Health Services.

Mindy confides in Meg about her desire to get STI testing and her request that Ronny use condoms in their sexual relationships. Meg listens carefully to Mindy and reviews with her the difficult choices she faces. She hears Mindy's ambivalence and anxiety. She also senses Mindy's vulnerability and loneliness. To provide Mindy with more time to process, Meg invites Mindy to return in a few days to continue the conversation. Meg sees the relief on Mindy's face when she knows that she can return soon to discuss an issue that is throwing off her sleep, concentration, and appetite.

Meg's value of the mentoring relationship is evident. Asking for what one deserves, which is what Mindy did, is a tool of resistance. Meg reminded Mindy of her life-affirming commitment to health. Although Mindy was dismissed by Ronny and others in her circle of friends, Meg validated Mindy's position. She reminded Mindy that people who care about one another do not ask their partners to abandon their values or throw away their rights. They negotiate, problem-solve, and work through the conflict. Being able to live freely and feel safe within a relationship is a reflection of justice. Mindy had every right to demand safety, as well as the freedom to choose and to say no. Ultimately, Meg was able to use her knowledge and wisdom as an adult woman and as a nurse to understand and support Mindy. She praised Mindy for refusing to self-silence and commended her mentee for understanding the health dangers of inadequate protection during sex and for being a champion of self-care.

As a Sister Resister, Meg did not claim to be the race or gender expert. Meg's ability to show up as a Sister Resister was influenced by her own narrative. She saw in her own past relationships, as well as among her women friends, the tendency to place their wants and personal preferences below those of their partners. Meg was injured by and resented such relational mistreatment, having seen far too many lives sidetracked when women acquiesced. She listened closely to Mindy without judgement. She created a validating environment as Mindy pushed back against a relationship that was dismissive and pushed through the agony of walking away from someone she cares about. While working across the visible social differences of age and race, Meg mentored with veracity, in a way that was honest, authentic, and intentional. Her value of Mindy's resistance led to the asking of relevant yet bold questions that resulted in her joining with her young mentee to live out loud and embrace her life on her own terms.

CHAPTER 5

Resistance and Mentoring Relationships

SUPPORTING HEALTHY RESISTANCE can be tough. Every Black student is an individual and the situations they face call for individualized attention. Resistance strategies work best when they are tailor-made for the circumstances at hand. Sometimes, White mentors may feel the need to reach out to other faculty, administrators, and staff for assistance in designing effective mentoring strategies with and on behalf of Black female students. Not surprisingly, some of the people Sister Resisters turn to are adult Black women or other women of color on campus in order to benefit from their wisdom and expertise. At times, these connections can be made effortlessly as BIPOC women might welcome being solicited for their help. The Black adult women on campus may feel appreciated and willing to share their cultural knowledge and successful strategies that they have constructed. But at other times, these requests for help solicited across lines of social differences might be met with skepticism, disinterest, and even anger. In those instances, the invitation to connect might be rebuffed—sometimes graciously, but at other times maybe not so.

The reasons for such resistance are numerous. Often the challenges that Black college students struggle with are also being navigated by the BIPOC adults on campus as well. On predominantly White campuses, Black faculty often find themselves racially isolated due to their very few numbers. Research suggests that similar to Black students, Black faculty and administrators also encounter racism both on and off campus. Black faculty report feeling their authority is challenged in the classroom by White students; they feel talked over and presumed incompetent in committee meetings with White colleagues, and their scholarship (particularly when it focuses on race and racism) is dismissed as subjective, politically tainted, and self-serving.[1] On campus, faculty of color may be mistaken for maintenance or cafeteria workers, and Black administrative staff report being ignored and their contributions demeaned. In these caustic environments, the last thing Black faculty want to do is bend over backward to explain racism to a mentor, especially when there is little evidence that the White colleague can hear and act on this truth. White colleagues need to recognize that sharing information with Black faculty about a racial event on campus can be particularly painful to the person who hears it. Not just because of the incidents described: often Black faculty know and experience these racially charged situations all too well. They have probably also lived them (or are currently living them). Hearing about such a situation from a well-meaning White colleague could trigger unpleasant memories filled with unresolved emotions. An invitation to listen (and an unspoken expectation to act) may feel like yet another burden White folks expect Black folks to take on. Many Black faculty are already overwhelmed with the often uncompensated extra work of serving on diversity, equity, and inclusion (DEI) committees, advising BIPOC students, and being expected to willingly participate in campus-led diversity and antiracism initiatives. In the absence of collegial respect and trust, it is foolhardy to expect people of color to collaborate.

Cultural Mistrust: Confronting Complicated Cross-Racial Relationships

We would be remiss if we avoided the deeply complicated matter of Black and White women's cross-racial interpersonal relationships on and off college campuses. Cross-racial conflict and mistrust has haunted and continues to damage our relational connections. Unfortunately, the ties that bind and separate Black and White women date back to our earliest beginnings in the United States. Over the past four hundred years, women's relationships (both inter- and intraracial) have been used to uphold patriarchy, racism, and other power inequities in the United States.[2] Our unbalanced social positions have obscured our racial realities, and that has created moments of invisibility and hyper-visibility that continue to shape how we see ourselves and each other. Historians have documented the difficulties Black and White women faced working together in the suffrage, civil rights, and women's libera-tion movements of the past.[3] Accusations of gendered racism, White supremacy, racial arrogance, and the refusal to listen to and integrate the concerns of Black women into movement agendas often led women to abandon the hope of building alliances across their differences. More often than not, the women in these movements chose instead to go their separate ways. Doing so ultimately impeded social progress. If we are not careful, our racial conflicts today will do the same.

Cultural mistrust can also play a disruptive role in the mentoring relationship. Young Black women's mistrust of White mentors reflects a psychologically adaptive function that operates to protect the Black woman's sense of self from harm and injury. The seeds of cultural mis-trust were probably planted well before the Black mentee and the White mentor ever met. Scholars explore the messages created and passed down within families, communities, and legacies that facilitate or block trust and interpersonal honesty between Black and White women. In many Black families, Black girls grow up hearing messages that cau-tion them that White people are untrustworthy. Other Black students enter college having had poor experiences with White female teachers in their earlier years of schooling, which also adds to difficulties in trust-building with White mentors. Once in college and assigned to a mentor, Black students may be reluctant to share their everyday experi-ences of microaggressions with their mentors, fearing that they will be invalidated or belittled when these events are brought to light. In these cases, Black women rarely feel safe as they fear that the worst of their suspicions will become affirmed: that their mentors are clueless and undependable.

Healthy cross-racial mentoring relationships understand and respect the sociopolitical, cultural, personal, and historical contexts of both the mentor and the mentee. Relationships with mentors who insist on being seen as knowledgeable yet are experienced by mentees as color evasive and racially fragile seldom contribute to positive outcomes. We have heard stories of mentors failing to honor confidential information that Black mentees had shared. At times, mentors minimize or dismiss what mentees see as important and problematic. We have even heard stories of mentors constantly seeking to fix things for Black students: swooping in like White saviors, hell-bent on repairing the racial injuries that they feel feckless Black students cannot. None of these situations are conducive to healthy cross-racial relationships, and they hardly set the stage for mentors and mentees to collaboratively partner in constructing resistance strategies that will improve Black students' lives.

Sister Resisters accept the task of deeply understanding and learning to overcome the conflicts that arise between women across their social differences. Due to our histories of social imbalance, there is a great deal of anger Black women have been forced to hold back, and many truths we have been forced to conceal. Collaboration between Sister Resisters working across race demands that women confront the lingering feelings of mistrust, hypocrisy, and frustration that exists between them. White and BIPOC Sister Resisters need to critically examine the dynamics of color blindness, racial minimization, and White fragility that interfere with authentic relational connections.

Despite this daunting information, critical, intentional, *and really good* mentoring that matters is possible. Cultural mistrust can be overcome. To do so requires first that mentors purposefully spend significant time getting to know their Black mentees. But that is just the first step. Overcoming cultural mistrust demands doing the work of interrogating Whiteness. It requires deepening one's understanding of racial history and exploring personal and collective identities. It requires examining the relationships among Whiteness, heterosexism, racism, and power. Here are a few things to pay attention to: Who do you invite to dinner at your house, and who is not around your table? Straight Black colleagues in couples? Gay couples? Neither? Creating the relational bonds necessary to forge strong and powerful alliances between young Black women and adult Sister Resisters requires the energizing forces that emerge from fearless determination and mutual courage.

Courage is needed by both women, but for different reasons. Black women need courage to resist disconnecting from White women out of fear, frustration, or as a habitual response. Allowing herself to trust White women, particularly when she is emotionally vulnerable and in need of support and care, requires a level of self-confidence and bravery from a young Black woman that must not be overlooked. White women, too, need their own measure of courage to bridge the relational divide. Courage is an antidote to fear, and it aids Sister Resisters in their effort to resist retreating into staying silent and "racially innocent" in the presence of racism, especially when among colleagues and friends. Courage energizes Sister Resisters. It fuels their resolve to deal with the overwhelming fatigue that will surely take hold as they fight for racial justice and insist that their Black female mentees are treated with fairness and respect.

Opposing Miseducation

Mentors rely on many skills when supporting students toward graduation. One such skill is to pay close attention to the mentee's experience of her educational program, especially when the path to success appears to be difficult to navigate. Students get derailed for any number of reasons, such as inadequate study habits, poor time-management skills, spotty attendance, and the like. Sister Resisters can add to this list that there might be a misalignment of curriculum relevance to the interests, needs, and experiences of the students enrolled in a department or program. This next story is about curricula truth telling and the recognition that sometimes what we teach in our college classrooms sidesteps difficult topics and lacks relevance to essential social realities, particularly when racial sensitivities are involved. A relevant curriculum is one that is meant to give students the opportunity to develop the vocational knowledge specific to the occupation for which they wish to qualify. But sometimes the courses we require students to take actually reveal knowledge gaps that leave students ill-prepared and diminish student engagement.

Paula is an advisor in the health sciences program and she knows the meaning of fighting for racial justice on campus. She heard her email ping and looked up at the computer screen. She groaned quietly as she read the message from her mentee's advisor. The notes on the academic chart read "late assignments," "minimal class engagement," and "too argumentative in class discussions." Apparently, Cheyenne was failing a class. Paula was surprised. Cheyenne's dream was to become a physician assistant (PA), and although she had struggled earlier with a few of the required science courses, Paula was impressed with Cheyenne's self-advocacy and persever-ance. She signed up for tutoring, attended study sessions, and stayed in close contact with her advisor and mentor throughout the semester.

In fact, that is how Paula came to really know her mentee. It was in those weekly conversations between the two women that Cheyenne talked at length about the absence of culturally specific information offered in her premed courses. From Cheyenne's perspective, racial matters and cul-tural differences were glossed over or completely ignored in class. Dispari-ties in health care were framed as "patient problems"—usually due to their lack of compliance, their ignorance, cultural disadvantage, or their "low socioeconomic status." Paula knew that Cheyenne wanted more. In her short life, Cheyenne had seen family members mistreated by medical per-sonnel. Levels of mistrust were so high in her community that sick neigh-bors would rather suffer at home than visit an unwelcoming clinic. Health care inequities such as these are what inspired Cheyenne to apply to the university's PA program in the first place.

Paula was determined to get Cheyenne through the PA program. Over the two years of their mentoring relationship, Cheyenne's career desire had become her own. Worried, the mentor called Cheyenne to her office to discuss the failing course. Immediately, her mentee burst into tears.

"These White professors just want to present the medical field as heroic and brave. They never want to talk about how their own attitudes and behaviors contribute to racial bias in health care delivery. They con-stantly ignore how racism is alive and well in medical care. This is *my* com-munity that they are blowing off! And the students in my class don't know enough to care. I've seen them roll their eyes when I start to speak. They don't even believe me when I tell them what I've seen: the grandmamas in my neighborhood who have to ration their insulin shots or the folks who don't return for follow-up because they can't afford the co-pay. Dismissing these problems as just 'ghetto problems' that these middle-class practitio-ners probably won't have to deal with in their worksites is dishonest and not an accurate reflection of how society looks. Why isn't this information as important as the other stuff we have to learn and get tested on? I've had it with these courses and these people who think they know everything."

Paula handed Cheyenne a tissue as she considered what she should say. She knew how passionate Cheyenne was about improving health care in her home community and she certainly wanted to support her professional goals. She also knew that sometimes what looks like disinterest or anger is the concealment of hurt and powerlessness. Before becoming Cheyenne's mentor, Paula hadn't spent much time interrogating the courses offered to students in the science programs. She had not considered the lack of representation or the cultural bias tied to whose values and interests were privileged or overlooked. This situation with Cheyenne convinced her that the cultural silences Cheyenne referenced were a real problem that should be addressed. Faculty instructors teach what they know, and if their knowledge of the impact of racism and sexism is absent or incomplete, the students are the ones who suffer.

Faculty who downplay structural racism in medicine and health care delivery ultimately fail to prepare our preservice students for the diverse patient populations they will face when they enter the profession. Too often academics (and the disciplines that they represent) are not held accountable for teaching information that has been found to be racist, sexist, or filled with historical, biological, and sociological errors and omissions. Studies of school textbooks show that these materials generally reflect mainstream Euro-American experiences and worldviews. Instructional practices in secondary and even college classrooms too often disconnect racism in the past from racism today. Some professors still frame racism as the act of a few bad individuals rather than a system of oppression. And challenges to racism in their respective fields, if attended to at all, are depicted as the actions of heroic individuals rather than organized struggle.[4] In many academic disciplines, the calls for substantive curriculum revision have gone unheeded, despite the fact that we live in a global world with increasing numbers of students across diversity entering our classrooms.

At the turn of the twentieth century, Black historian Carter G. Woodson identified what he labeled as the *miseducation* of students in our classrooms. Philosopher Audrey Thompson, building on Woodson's notion of miseducation, warns that curricular falsification "misprepares students for the actual social conditions that they are likely to encounter. It misrepresents knowledge . . . and lies to students about who they are or what their society is like."[5] Sister Resisters keep an eye out for such distortions. They cultivate a racial consciousness that acknowledges the ways in which racism can be denied, minimized, and justified in higher education institutions. Sister Resisters uncover the truth. Their veracity is a tool for advocacy on behalf of Black women on campus.

Paula used her power to name the exclusionary instructional practices that diminish the importance of race and racism in students' professional training. By calling for a more inclusive, antiracist curricular approach, she resisted miseducating college and university students in their institution. Together, Paula and her mentee Cheyenne decided to co-construct a multitiered and holistic resistance response. They searched the university course catalog for an elective Cheyenne could take that focused specifically on race and medicine. They talked with her departmental advisor about interning in a neighborhood clinic to enhance her practice skills. Finally, they arranged for Cheyenne to meet regularly with an alumnus from the university, another Black woman now working in the field who was happy to take on a preservice mentee from her previous program. Paula knew that there are times when a Black mentee needs more than one mentor. Finding another Black woman with whom Cheyenne could share her racialized experiences in the program and learn to navigate race-based challenges in the field would provide Cheyenne the educational training she needed and deserved.

Mentoring with Peers

The following case is a departure from previous case studies in this book. Most of the attention has been on the mentor-mentee dyad. However, when resistance practice requires Sister Resisters to work closely with colleagues, some of whom may also be in mentoring capacities and others not, decision-making regarding effective resistance may become more complicated.

Brenda is a financial aid counselor at a large university. She is an American-born White woman and has been married for seven years to Ken, an African American man. They have a daughter who is five years old. Brenda met Sheila, a colleague from another area in her college, about a year ago at a DEI training, and the two women developed a casual friendship. Sheila identifies as a Black, South African–born woman. Both mothers enjoy sharing stories, particularly those of their children's development. In the middle of a story about grooming her daughter's hair, Brenda blurted out to her friend, "I don't know how I am going to tame my daughter's wild hair. I'm thinking about cutting it all off so that I don't start looking like a muscle-bound athlete after wrestling with that girl's hair every day." At first Sheila hesitated, then she asked Brenda, "Why do you make those kinds of statements? Aren't you worried that your daughter will grow up feeling badly about her body? Her thick, kinky hair tells a story of her African heritage. Do you not see its beauty?" Surprised and embarrassed, Brenda quipped defensively, "I am married to a Black man, I have a very brown child, and last summer, I marched for Black Lives Matter. I didn't make it as far as I have in this office without understanding gender discrimination, and I am the last person in this room who could be called racist!"

Brenda considers herself to be politically conscious, socially aware, and more racially developed than most of her White friends and acquaintances. Marriage to a Black man and mothering a biracial child is, to Brenda, evidence of her identity as nonracist. She feels compelled to remind her Black friend of these points. But Sheila, in her wisdom, does not see it that way. Sheila knows that such intimate relationships are neither exculpation nor absolution from the values and beliefs of White supremacist thought. She worries about what can happen when White women think that they know all there is to know about how racism operates. From Sheila's perspective, Brenda's attitude suggests a noticeable lack of cultural humility. She thinks her own understanding of the experiences of Black people is complete and that she has little else to learn. Moreover, embedded in Brenda's defensiveness is a sense of herself as knowledgeable about racism and sexism, a knowledge stance that she feels renders her blameless. In her mind, the fact that she has experienced gender bias makes it impossible to be guilty of participating in any systems of sexism and racism. The problem is that in seeing gender inequality as equivalent to racial injustice, Brenda overlooks the fact that the two are far from the same. Most importantly, Brenda has yet to recognize that her daughter will be up against both forces in her life. Her lack of understanding of gendered racism invalidates her daughter's experiences, and Sheila worries that she will bring the same incomprehension to the experiences of the Black college women she mentors.

For more White women, being admonished about racial issues by Black women is hard to hear, particularly women who imagine themselves to be antiracist. These women are quick to claim they have marched for social justice or that they have a Black friend, a Black partner, and/or a biracial child. Such relationships hardly make one immune from the toxicity of racism. In fact, Brenda's lack of insight makes her blind to how racism has shaped her thinking. Her view of racism suggests a fully inaccurate understanding of how the system operates. When racism is associated with acts of interpersonal meanness, it is easy to extract oneself from the workings of racial oppression: *If I have a Black partner and friend, then I am not a racist.* Her sense of herself as a morally good person allows her to believe: *I can't harbor racist thoughts or behave in a racist manner.* What Brenda doesn't see is that her worldview and self-image is imbued with racial arrogance and superiority: *I don't have to listen to a Black woman who contradicts my position.* And two things are particularly sad and disappointing here. First, Brenda is unable to acknowledge and accept that despite the fact that she is the mother of a multiracial family, she still has more to learn. There is a good chance that Brenda's lack of insight regarding her own race- and gender-blind spots may become problematic for the Black female students with whom she has a mentoring relationship. Second, this short interaction may have caused a breach within Sheila and Brenda's friendship. Such relational injuries are known to occur when White women are unable and unwilling to see what is brought to their attention, especially when the critique comes from the mouths of Black women.

Suboptimal Resistance

White women mentors who endeavor to join with Black college mentees to resist racism and other forms of societal oppression in their lives are up against some formidable foes. The work of resistance is risky, rough, and unrelenting. For White women, it can be surprising and healing to learn that the work of antiracism is for the long haul. It requires self-forgiveness, plus acceptance that you have made and will make more mistakes. We have been told by White women colleagues attempting to be antiracist that they often see Black women colleagues as gentler and more understanding. They have said that Black women are more willing to listen to their White coworkers when they feel they are really trying, and they are more forgiving than the White faculty members may be of themselves. Self-critique and self-doubt among women on the journey to antiracism can be vicious. Mentors will make errors, and because mistakes are inevitable (and reflect our collective humanity), it is paramount for mentors to be conscious and accepting of their missteps. They should always have at their disposal a reparative tool kit with which they can redress whatever inadvertent miscalculations were made as they work to support the success of their Black female mentees.

When helping Black college women navigate through the array of systemic oppressions blocking their way, mentors may find that choosing the most effective resistance strategy can be a complicated endeavor. As we have shown earlier, mentees themselves do not always make the best decisions regarding the manner of resistance they think will work best. Similarly, when considering the available options, mentors also may mistakenly employ strategies of resistance that we describe as *suboptimal*. *Suboptimal resistance* refers to situations in which mentors understand the importance of resistance in the psychosocial development of Black female students, but rather than being liberatory, resilience-building, and self-affirming, the resistance strategies that the mentor recommends fall short on one or more levels.[6] Working within our framework of detecting and naming social inequities, we've seen mentors stumble when it becomes time for a Black mentee to effectively oppose the oppression that stands in her way. Missteps can occur in any number of ways. A mentor may fail to appreciate that a strategy that works for one group of women may not work nearly as well for women from another social group. Take, for example, a Black queer student who is experiencing interpersonal conflict in a Black student organization that feels homophobic and unwelcoming. To a mentor, it might make sense to encourage the student to hang in there—but this is unfair to ask of a Black queer student for whom remaining in that environment might be too painful. Similarly, if the Black student organization feels more like an elite sorority than an activist space, mentors need to know that some queer students and working-class students may not feel embraced.

And as we showed in Brenda's case, a mentor's misstep might conflate her personal marginalized identity with being nonracist (when this is not the case).

In the following narrative, suboptimal resistance occurs when a White mentor makes two key misjudgments: First, her suggestions are rooted in a White racial frame that ignores the significance of her mentee's intersectional identities and the impact that race as a grand master status can inflict on the matter at hand. Second, the mentor suggests a resistance action but fails to anticipate the resulting consequences BIPOC people may suffer when they act on the advice she is offering.

Parker, who identifies as *they*, is a Black LGBTIQ mentee. They are experimenting with different attire to fit their evolving identity: replacing the dresses they had worn to an off-campus work-study site last semester with more genderless, unisex attire. Parker's White mentor, Tam, who is also LGBTIQ, is excited that Parker is finding their voice. She encourages her mentee to resist conventional standards of dress expected for women and choose instead to wear what they want. But not everyone sees these decisions in the same way. At the site, Parker is mocked, sometimes to their face, and one day they discover that their car tires were slashed.

Tam was shocked at the violence that Parker encountered at the worksite. What she came to realize is that by encouraging Parker's defiant resistance to gender conformity, she had narrowly focused on only one aspect of her mentee's identity. In so doing she had overlooked the primacy of race. Resistance to patriarchy without attention to the intersectionality of queerness, race, and physical presentation can be especially dangerous for a Black mentee. Tam, the mentor, was well aware of the stigmatized identities that she and her mentee shared and the animus toward queer individuals that makes the world an unwelcoming place for them both. This was the knowledge Tam used, both to establish solidarity with Parker and to offer wisdom from her experiences and beliefs. But, Tam discovered, those identity connections did not render her immune from minimizing race and racism in Parker's life.

Tam learned an essential lesson in resisting across differences. Her resistance is not the same as her mentee's resistance. The oppression faced by both women may overlap in important ways, but undeniable differences still remain. Resistance for Black women cannot singularly focus on the same struggles White women confront without also addressing the multiple oppressions faced specifically by women with darker skin. In the future, Tam would be wise to figure out how to center her mentee's needs when supporting their efforts to effectively resist. All of us operate under conditions of Whiteness and patriarchy; therefore Tam needs to always remember that White women, if not careful, can reproduce the very oppressions they assumed they were resisting.

Meanwhile, Tam and her mentee can help change the culture on campus by sponsoring a well-known Black trans activist, organizing panel discussions, or in some other way creating a buzz that can help shift consciousness. Together, the mentor and mentee can create a shared historical memory by cosponsoring an event and collaborating on making the campus more inclusive.

The Uses of Power and Privilege

The following case illustrates the importance of Sister Resisters being willing to advise, model for, and join with other White colleagues and women mentors in the service of mentoring Black college women. Here we highlight the significance of Black mentees having more knowledge than their mentors about the significance of race. We also see how peer mentoring can benefit adult women in their growth and skill development.

Ahmeda is a twenty-year-old rising junior in college who is applying for internship positions. Her family immigrated to the United States from Eritrea. She has lived in the US since 2007, when she arrived at age thirteen. Ahmeda read in a social studies class about research documenting that employers often discriminate against job candidates on the basis of their names and the employers' perceptions of the candidate's race. Ahmeda mentioned the study when she met with her mentor Susan. She said, "I am not changing my name for anybody! Why should I be ashamed of who I am? If people don't want to hire me because they suspect that I'm Muslim and a Black African woman, then I do not want to do my internship there." Susan was not sure of the best way to respond to Ahmeda, so she brought up the interaction with her colleague Lila at lunch. Both are White and American-born and are volunteer members of the university's mentoring program. Susan explained, "I am pleased that Ahmeda is proud of her name and nationality. Changing her name so that a racist employer can't identify her as a Black female who might also be Muslim does not mean she is ashamed of herself. But I can't help thinking that if she called herself Amy, doors would open to her faster than using her given name, Ahmeda. I know she did not create this racist society, and I know it's not fair, but I want her to forget about that silliness and secure this internship."

Lila listened carefully to her colleague. After thinking through her response to Susan, she replied, "It is really great that Ahmeda is able to speak so freely with you about racial injustice and I'm glad that you are helping her make sense of the racism—what you call 'the silliness' at that worksite. But if she took your advice and changed her name to Amy, what else would she have to change to fit into a system that is dictated by White racist norms? We do not want Ahmeda to erase who she is. Will straightening her hair be next or fixing her nose or not wearing her hijab? My concern is that Ahmeda alone is burdened with the responsibility of combating racism. That's not right. I wonder if we could do some training with our internship sites about the findings from these research studies and the biases associated with ethnic-sounding names? Maybe if we do that, we'll be making structural changes against racism instead of leaving the hard work to our students of color by just giving lip service to diversity and equity. Does that make sense? Is that something you think the two of us can take on?"

As we have often noted throughout this book, becoming an intentional mentor requires ongoing self-examination, antiracism knowledge, and a commitment to pushing back against social bias and standing up for equity. Attaining these skills takes time and requires a great deal of trial and error. It is hard work. Through collaboration with White colleagues, White women have an opportunity to deepen their skills for resisting gendered racism. We argue that White women are in a better position to impart this knowledge to other White women who may struggle with receiving instruction and race-related critique from BIPOC women. White women may find it hard to accept feedback from Black women and in particular from a younger, presumed-inexperienced mentee.

At the start of their conversation, Susan and Lila did not share the same depth of understanding about how racial, gender, and religious bias are at play in this situation. As a social justice advocate, Lila has learned to "read" situations like these as a first step to determine how best to respond. When Lila spoke up to Susan, she knew she was taking a calculated risk. She sensed that she might be walking into the hornet's nest of emotional responses that are triggered in many White people when they are made aware of their racial biases.[7] It has been her experience that conversations about racism, as a fugitive topic, heightens anxiety and gives rise to defensiveness, making race talk something White Americans prefer to avoid. At the same time, Lila knew there were other matters to consider when she chose to use her voice. White individuals who speak up from a stage of racial consciousness that differs from those around them may find themselves in the unenviable position of being relationally disconnected, ostracized, and rejected by their peers. For these reasons, Lila proceeds thoughtfully as she executes her next moves. She carefully monitors both her language and emotional reaction to hearing Susan's reference to the situation as "silly." She looks for the patterns of racism—in this case, how ethnic names can be weaponized to serve the interests of others. Susan's suggestion that her mentee take the easy way out and change her name, from Lila's vantage point, is a White racial frame of reference, one that "circulates and reinforces racial messages that position Whites as superior."[8] Lila named the message as a form of racism—an elevation of White-sounding names above all others. Changing the name *Ahmeda* to *Amy*, Lila believes, reinforces the idea that White names and White culture are preferred and are more appropriate in a professional setting.[9]

Now, it is possible that Susan imagined Ahmeda's name change was a clever and expedient way to skirt the system. She may even have innocently imagined that Ahmeda's name change was an appropriate act of resistance, an easy step her mentee could take to avoid racial/ethnic devaluation. But what Susan missed is what Ahmeda would be giving up in the process. Personal and family names are steeped in meaning and tradition. In many cultural communities, names are a primary identity marker, deliberated over and considered very carefully before they are bestowed upon a child. The act of naming is often connected to people's ancestry, land, memory, religion, and spiritual practices. To many people around the world, names tie individuals to the past in ways that cannot be swapped out like a fashion accessory. The idea of changing one's name to something more White-like in order for others to be able to say it without effort (and for them to avoid being reminded that other names and cultures actually exist) might, in Susan's eyes, be seen as a resistance strategy. But the solution it calls for is short term and survival oriented. It might solve the problem in the moment, but it doesn't affirm who Ahmeda is as a Black Muslim woman. Therefore, it fails the test of reflecting optimal resistance.

Susan's orientation reflects an imposition of power, the type that reinforces for Ahmeda a worldview that exemplifies suboptimal or unhealthy resistance. Despite being well-meaning, her actions were racially oppressive. Susan's suggestion fails to support Ahmeda's identity in that it devalues her Muslim religion and buys into notions of White racial/cultural superiority and anti-Blackness. Thankfully, Ahmeda's statement of refusing to work in spaces that seek to erase her identity reflects her healthy inclination to push back and resist. Yet as brave as Ahmeda is, she needs the support of a mentor like Lila—a Sister Resister who will support her opposition to self-erasure and her refusal to prop up a hurtful system steeped in Whiteness.

Susan could come to acknowledge her biases and prejudices, but most likely not by herself. Susan needs a peer mentor.[10] With Lila's intervention, we hope that Susan could better understand her own behavior. And if Susan accepts Lila's invitation to visit her mentee's worksite, Susan's understanding of what effective resistance looks like may even strengthen. Lila immediately recognizes the role she could play in challenging institutional racism at the site where students complete their internships. University faculty who work with community-based organizations and other outside institutions are in a position to educate these agencies about unintentional bias and the imposition of Whiteness on BIPOC people. Recognizing that working to upend racism must be their primary goal, Lila spoke honestly with Susan about true allyship. She suggested to her colleague that together they should use their privilege and power to disrupt racially charged institutional practices, thereby ensuring that the doors of access are open equitably to all of their students.

In addition to interpersonal conflict, there are also possible institutional implications at play. Hearing critical feedback from university faculty about their institutional practices may make the internship site confused, defensive, and even indignant. Fear of losing this contract could push some mentors to choose silence and maintain the status quo. Anger and disappointment could be displaced onto Susan and quite possibly onto the higher educational institution that she represents. Speaking up can jeopardize her employment status, income, and benefits. Resisting institutional bias has its own complications and possible consequences that one would be foolish to ignore.

Our model of resistance beckons White women to challenge and question practices, policies, and politics that label all things Black as inferior and all things White as preferable. As a Sister Resister, it was a smart move for Lila to ask Susan to recover and reclaim her agency as a social justice advocate. Lila helped Susan to see that in supporting Ahmeda's decision to decline employment in a job that prefers that she Whitewash her identity for the comfort of others, she too is learning how to resist on behalf of the Black mentees in her charge. This time it was Ahmeda (the mentee) who taught Susan (the mentor) to never dishonor one's intrinsic self-worth. As we have stated many times, a Sister Resister who joins the resistance is growing as well. She is learning to appreciate the cultural wealth of Black women's moral authority; this includes knowing how and why Black women feel it necessary to resist those who would devalue them. Better yet, Susan is learning how to support Black women in those moments when they do so. She is expanding her knowledge of how racism operates in White institutions (usually behind the scenes and below the radar of other White people) and, with Lila's urging, how to use one's power and privilege to educate others for social change. We trust here that Susan's ability to resist effectively is actively developing and that she may be inspired to become a social justice warrior because of her work with both Lila and Ahmeda.

Psychologist Janet Helms writes that "for racism to disappear in the United States, White people must take the responsibility for ending it. For them to assume that responsibility, they must become aware of how racism hurts White people and consequently how ending it serves White people's interests. Moreover, this awareness not only must be accompanied by enhanced abilities to recognize the many faces of racism, but also by the discovery of options to replace it."[11]

A Sister Resister collaborates with Black students, faculty, and staff by calling her colleagues out when necessary. She helps them to see what they could and should do differently and why their microaggressions, unexamined cultural assumptions, and inability to acknowledge bias in words and deeds really matter. She uses her privilege to assist and advocate, knowing that to do so will require courage, personal fortitude, and an unwavering commitment to the ongoing work of achieving social justice for all of the students that she has been hired to serve.

It has been our experience that White women who adopt a Sister Resister stance will embrace the requisite attitudes and behaviors necessary to become a resistance collaborator with their colleagues of color. Collaborating is not the same thing as passing the buck or finding someone else to do your work for you. Sister Resisters can build meaningful relationships with Black women and other BIPOC men and women on campus who are able to provide productive spaces for collaboration. This requires that Sister Resisters commit to doing their homework—educating themselves about issues on campus that BIPOC members in their college community are dealing with. It also requires that they resist those who insist on avoiding conversations of racial bias in the community or who insist on projecting an image of being color-blind or, as is more common these days, an image of being antiracist and "woke." She must practice resisting effectively, efficiently, and appropriately with and on behalf of those who may need her help to do so. To that end, once Susan has done the work of educating herself about Muslim women and resistance, she could give her mentee books and references about Muslim women who have wrestled with and confronted xenophobia and Islamophobia. Doing so would reinforce the synergistic link between activism and critical intellectual studies and open a space for further conversation between mentors and mentees.[12]

Some Final Thoughts About Mentoring for Resistance

In the case of White Sister Resisters who find themselves mentoring Black female students in the absence of adult Black women or other women of color, the work of resistance requires even greater finesse. These women may be working in overwhelmingly White regions of the country or in departments or in colleges within a university where there are very few faculty, administrators, or staff of color. In these settings, Sister Resisters may be told by their White colleagues, "I don't have any Black students, so what does this antiracist work have to do with me?" More often, Sister Resisters may find themselves face to face with other White colleagues who assume that people of color (and only people of color) can, should, and are best suited to work with Black students, especially around issues of gendered racial bias and belonging. What is seldom admitted or expressed out loud is that many White professionals feel ill-equipped to take on this work. They feel it is not their job, or they sense that they don't know how to mentor in the ways we have described. Rather than give up, this is exactly when our Sister Resisters need to double down and reject the impedance from their colleagues with all they've got.

Sister Resisters must become comfortable pushing against the powers that be. They have to become comfortable with failure and accustomed to incremental change taking far longer than they believe it should. They must accept that sometimes they will have to wait. They may find themselves alienated from other White people who disagree with their acts of allyship. Not everyone will appreciate being called out for a microaggression and may resent charges of bias in decision-making protocols. Sister Resisters must be ready for the faulty accusations proclaiming that they are the ones perpetuating racism and making mountains out of molehills for political gain. They may even be accused of choosing sides.

White women who make these commitments run the risk of being denied promotions, left out of crucial White decision-making circles, and denied committee elections. So, you may ask, why do it? Because your life will become more purposeful. Because students of color will enrich your life. Because racism does not just hurt Black people; racism harms White people as well. And because authentic, relational, and connected community heals. A few small doors may close, but a whole world will open up.

Despite the opposition directed their way, Sister Resisters are exactly where they need to be. Mentoring for these women is focused and intentional. The work calls on women to listen and learn as they guide others and while developing themselves. In their mentoring practice, they nurture a particular kind of moral capacity, one that strengthens the dialectic between resistance and resilience and fosters a womanist ethic of care.

CHAPTER 6

Sister Resisters Rising

W E WRITE THIS BOOK during an unprecedented time in our nation's history. We have been hit by unrelenting waves of crises: a worldwide pandemic that nearly shut down the economy and took the lives of more than three-quarters of a million individuals in the US, plus large-scale protests expressing outrage at the horrifying deaths of George Floyd, Ahmaud Arbery, Breonna Taylor, Daunte Wright, Andrew Brown Jr., and many other Black people at the hands of police sworn to protect and serve. What began as a social media hashtag, #BlackLives-Matter, exploded into a global network of street protests against police brutality and systemic racism in American institutions. It has been said that this is a year of racial reckoning, and there have been increasing calls for citizens to *talk* to one another about racism, especially among young millennial populations. In our call to action, we go further. This book is not just focused on our need to talk about racism. We maintain that it is critical to talk *clearly*, *competently*, and *confidently* about racism. We also argue that learning to effectively respond to racism is equally as important as talking about it.

Resistance is a life jacket. It protects Black women from being drowned by the devastating forces of gendered racism. It enables Black women to stay afloat amid the inevitable tides of racism that batter the mind and body. Resistance fuels the indignation we feel to forge through, to push back against those who undermine our right to live our best lives—not the lives that others have imposed upon us. Resistance strengthens our ability to battle the violence of institutional and interpersonal racism. The act of reconciling racial expectations with racial reality and developing strategies to support this work creates a unity of purpose and resolve between the Black mentee and her Sister Resister mentor.

But Black women cannot and should not be expected to do this mighty work alone on our college campuses. Frankly, most Black students don't. They support and rely on each other, offering advice and providing encouragement to the best of their abilities. Consider, however, how their resistance could be strengthened with the assistance of an empowered Sister Resister. An adult woman who grasps what Black women in our culture are truly up against is golden as these women maneuver their way through the rugged racial and gendered terrain of university life. The effective mentor drinks from the well of her own wisdom, drawing lessons from her history of resistance against sexism (and all other relevant oppressions impacting her life). She is ready for this position, having integrated her self-knowledge with her knowledge of the inner workings of the institution.

Sister Resisters are able to read an environment for racial bias much like her mentees do. She has the courage to name and address racism where and when she sees it—even racism that lurks and seeks to hide from detection. Resisters know this is not about completely eliminating the racism that has been foundational to the reign of the Western world. Instead, Sister Resisters acknowledge that racism is shapeshifting and that they must be ready to respond as the situation demands. Rising against the forces of domination must be unfaltering. The path forward is not always clear, and fear will be a companion along the way—but with each successful resistance response, we rewire our brains. We create new memories. We remember the reason for our struggle and press forward. We become more resolute in our motivation to not be turned around.

Black Women's Resistance Tools

When we become aware of our oppression, the natural impulse is to resist. How we resist, whether it be in response to an incident of discrimination or a racially charged situation, calls for the use of responsible response strategies. Strategy adoption depends on the situation, the persons involved, the power dynamics at play, and the calculus one makes regarding consequences to the self when adopting a particular resistance response.

Managing racism and sexism is complicated. How we perceive and react to situations depends on personality traits and temperament, our analysis of the threat involved, our histories with trauma, coping capacities, and a host of other internal and external resources. Many people manage racial stress privately. Others rely on the support of family and friends. Some of us need the assistance of professional counselors and clinicians. The tool kit we describe in the following sections comprises a range of skills, including decision-making capacities and problem-solving techniques, the emotional intelligence required to handle race-based affect and resolve race-based conflicts, a strong self-concept, racial self-efficacy, sociopolitical awareness, cultural knowledge, and the ability to self-advocate.

Young people who face multiple adversities hunger for adults who are purposeful in helping them develop the competencies needed to sharpen their internal and external resources for academic and personal success. Throughout this book, we have identified the negative impact of gender bias, ethnic prejudice, and racial discrimination. And we believe that Black college students can acquire skills for transformation and empowerment. We trust they can feel competent in applying lessons of resistance and resilience, cultural pride, and critical consciousness from caring adults who are able to show up consistently as aware, honest, and attentive to issues of race, power, and injustice. They know, too, that resistance and resilience are elements of what psychologists refer to as *moral competence*—the ability to assess and respond to the ethical, affective, or social justice dimensions of a situation.[1] These elements of social and emotional health are essential given the persistence and intensity of structural inequities that frame the lives of BIPOC students, particularly those who are low income, first generation, LGBTIQ, living with intellectual and physical disabilities, religious minorities, and/or members of recently arrived Black immigrant populations. Ultimately, when students operationalize resistance, they develop strategies to reduce racial stressors, promote positive ethnic racial identity, and encourage healthy and emotional self-efficacy, as well as the capacity to handle positive and negative emotional experiences. These culturally informed approaches build on the wisdom and strengths that many Black women already bring to the college campus.

We seek to dismantle the hierarchical barriers that exist in traditional mentoring relationships. By making their perspectives and voices audible, Black female college students become knowledge producers. In sharing what they know, they author their own narratives with their Sister Resisters, and this interaction creates a new type of intentional mentoring. We identify the specific skills needed to construct effective resistance responses and offer suggestions for their implementation. Returning to our four-dimensional model—*see it, name it, oppose it,* and *replace it*—we integrate resistance affect, action, and awareness that support the application of each dimension.

Becoming an active resister is a tough assignment, one that requires personal fortitude, risk-taking, and a willingness to make mistakes. Mistakes can be challenging in the academy, given its focus on positivism and perfectionism. Nonetheless, vulnerability and humility are critical to resistance, as is faith in one's ability to keep trying. The liberatory contributions of our resistance model as a key developmental competency are evident from Clonan-Roy, Jacobs, and Nakkula, who write: "Many facets of the resistance competency, such as practicing resistance for liberation, operate as self-righting tendencies or protective practices that allow one to persevere through adversity and challenging experiences."[2] Resistance and resilience reinforce and empower each other. The strength to do both comes from multiple sources: self-awareness, cultural knowledge, faith and spirituality, and a commitment to social justice ideals. These lessons have been learned from those who fought oppression before us, and they can be taught to those of us who are engaged in these battles today.

Reflections on Resistance

Who are these strategies for? Black female college students are the primary population addressed in this book. We see these women constructing resistance strategies either independently or with their mentors. Because we acknowledge the impact of racism and the role of conscious and unconscious bias and discrimination in the lives of many students outside of the Black community, we believe that this information can be relevant to students who inhabit other stigmatized identities as well.

Why are strategies of resistance so important? Simply being aware of racism is not nearly enough. Black women must be able to cope effectively and manage the negative effects of this powerful force. Skills built upon social and psychological resistance capacities allow Black women to navigate the injustices and inequities that can impede success during the college years. Many children of African descent grew up in families or communities where conversations about recognizing racism and standing up to racially stressful encounters were commonplace. They received the requisite tools of resistance—the ability to read, name, and oppose racial microaggressions, biases, and unfair treatment. But as we have argued in these pages, such prior preparation may not have occurred for all Black college women. Our model provides the broad contours of the constitutive elements that Black women might consider and apply when confronted with negating stereotypes, the low expectations of others, and similar race- and gender-based invalidations.

Where should these strategies be used? Resistance strategies may be called for in classrooms, in residential dormitories, and in other venues on campus; in interactions with faculty and staff; and in on- and off-campus internships connected to college learning.

When should students apply strategies of resistance and what should they resist against? The list of what to resist is long, and it is closely connected to both the specific individual and the psychological state or social situation she is resisting. Black women are compelled to resist when they discern that their identity is under assault. In the college classroom, navigating microaggressions, dealing with colorblind ideologies, and exposure to cultural myths, mistruths, and misunderstandings are just a few examples. So too is believing that one is being treated unfairly or sensing that one's culture is being denigrated or ignored. Resistance is demanded when Black women feel victimized by misogynoir—that form of anti-Black sexism that discriminates against them in ways that are wholly unique.[3] Other instances that call for a resistance stance include Black women's encounters with patriarchal values that hold women back or White supremacist values and beliefs that elevate White womanhood above all other women. This book has only scratched the surface of the range of racially injurious policies, practices, politics, and interpersonal encounters Black women face in college life.

How should students resist? We encourage Black women in college to think critically about who they are and their place in the world so that they can sculpt a response appropriate to their racial reality. Creating effective resistance responses requires clear decision-making, conflict resolution, racial literacy, emotional regulation, and self-agency. These skills allow resisters to read racially charged situations as they emerge, then identify, name, and react responsibly to the routines of everyday racism and sexism that block their paths.

> "Why is it that every time the course readings address an issue regarding race, the professor always turns to me first for my opinion and to get the conversation started? Why always the Black student? Don't these White students have a race too?"

Reading situations for race entails observing, listening for, and picking up on patterns of discriminatory bias. Much like students learn to read a text, critical thinking skills are needed for this task of reading a racially charged event, breaking things down, examining its parts, and thinking about how the parts fit together. Sometimes, moving beyond the immediate situation is required. For example, it is a good idea to talk to other students in the class to hear their opinion and whether their assessments match one's own. What we have learned in our studies listening closely to Black college women is that the impact of gendered racism evokes strong emotional responses, and these emotions are key survival signals in that they indicate something important is happening. *Emotional knowledge*—"the ability to understand emotions—is related to social and behavioral outcomes and it is an important component of emotional regulation, expression, and perspective taking."[4] Possessing the capacity to be aware of, control, and express one's racialized emotions is emotional knowledge, and these are important skills that assist the decision-making that will emerge.

> *Mentee:* "I hate that lab instructor. She always has something to say when I arrive to class. I mean, yeah—I'm a little late, but what's the big deal. I'm

not a morning person, and that class starts at 8:30 a.m. I keep sleeping through the alarm. She stays on my back—always picking on me. I think she doesn't like me cuz I'm Black."

Mentor: "Maybe she doesn't like that you keep arriving late to her class."

Mentee: "So, what am I supposed to do?"

Mentor: "How about showing up on time. In fact, let's do this. Show up on time for four classes in a row. Let's see how she reacts. If she's still picking on you, I'll be the first in line to speak to her. But we first need to know what we're dealing with here."

Naming refers to the process of establishing criteria for determining if racism (or sexism) is, or is not, at play. Naming it requires practical, accessible words whose meanings are shared and understood. It means bringing the existence of injustice and inequity into full consciousness: *telling it like it is.* Sociopolitical knowledge, such as having an understanding of how racism works on the multiple levels in which it operates—interpersonal, systemic, and cultural—is foundational to the work of naming. The critical thinking skills we inculcate in college (deep intellectual interrogation and investigation, social analysis, critical consciousness, and political critique) inspire Black students to become aware of the falsifications, omissions, and distortions found in White-centered curricula and extra-curricular practices.[5]

Naming the racist content of a given situation requires discernment skills that assist Black women to think carefully about what they see, hear, think, believe, and feel. These skills allow them to determine if something in the situation is or is not racism or sexism and what situational element might bring harm. Not everything is about racism, and having the ability to call it accurately or to know when to seek some other explanation can be critical to a student's success, as illustrated in the preceding dialogue. But when the call is made, emotions flare and we feel the need to react. Coming face to face with actual racism, finding oneself embroiled in a racist act or the victim of someone's racist attitudes or behavior, can be frightening. Feeling oneself to be the casualty of somebody else's racism also produces anger, frustration, and disillusionment. Any one of these emotions could rise up and cloud one's judgment at the very moment when shrewd, clear-headed decision-making is required. Figuring out how to handle a racially charged interpersonal interaction judiciously calls for emotional coping strategies, an essential skill in the resistance tool set.

Finding smart and effective ways for Black women to mount a directed opposition to racism and sexism is at the heart of the resistance work we've described. *Opposing* race and gender oppression means standing up, fighting back, speaking up, and asserting moral authority. This means deciding what is right and standing up for it in the face of injustice, intolerance, and ignorance. The way one resists could be externally focused—for example, participating in protest marches to challenge racial injustice or engaging in other forms of advocacy work, like letter writing, circulating petitions, organizing social media campaigns, and participating in campus-led antiracist programming. Fostering partnerships with fellow resisters can also be included on this list. Likewise, the focus of the resistance could be internally directed—for example, shoring up one's resolve by fortifying oneself from within. This might mean educating oneself about a topic if a gap in one's knowledge exists, making a shift in how one is thinking about the situation, or changing something that one is or is not doing. And then there are the everyday resistance responses, like choosing to wear an Afrocentric natural hair style or refusing to change your ethnic-sounding name. Whatever the selected resistance response, it will require strategic problem-solving techniques that build on one's ability to imagine and carry out a process that will address issues and resolve the race-related dilemma at hand.

We have found it helpful to encourage Black women to think about the resistance strategies and tactics that others have used in the past. What worked and why? What didn't work, and why was that response unsuccessful? When discussing resistance choices, power analyses inevitably demand attention. Resisters must ask themselves: Who has the power here? What kind of power do they have, and how might it affect me? Whose interests are being privileged, favored, and legitimized, and whose interests are discounted, silenced, and ignored? What risks might there be to me should I oppose this exercise of power? And if there are risks, what is the best way for me to proceed?

We talk with Black college women about learning how to speak up in ways that increase their chances of being heard. What some call *passionate*, others label as *wild* and *aggressive*, particularly when the words and the tone used to convey the message come from Black women. Thus, communication style differences and the perceptions Black women might be up against is an important factor to consider when deciding on a resistance response. And let's be honest: not all Black students share the same opinions about struggling against White supremacy in their college years. We are not all united in solidarity. We do not all agree on how to, or even that we should, resist the notions of Whiteness that we have internalized. Resisters need to know this reality as they seek allies and make allegiances with others when necessary. Learning how to build consensus with others is as important as learning how to successfully negotiate racial conflict when it comes up. These conversations promote the idea that the work of resistance is multifaceted, ongoing, and never-ending. The game plan is straightforward: pick up on patterns, see what works, adapt it to one's own circumstances, analyze whether it was successful, and, if not, readjust your strategy for the next time.

In determining the best route forward, resisters must recognize that some oppositional attitudes and behaviors might be problematic, short-sighted, misguided, and survival oriented. Such poorly chosen responses might ultimately keep Black students trapped in the subordinate position they were initially trying to avoid. Opposing involves crafting effective and efficient resistance strategies customized for the specific circumstances being addressed. Because resisters are often called upon to create a strategy where one doesn't yet exist, they need to have a wide repertoire of available strategies at their disposal. When standing up to injustice, the best route forward is the path that encourages Black women to embrace the liberatory channels of academic achievement, self-determination, positive identity affirmation (individual, racial, ethnic, and gender), and racial pride. Finally, Black resisters are goal setters, and we urge them to evaluate the long-term impact of any decisions they choose. Missteps are common. We all make mistakes. Resisters are mindful of the consequences that might befall them when missteps occur in their lives. Such positive healthy resistance is at the root of envisioning an empowering future with long-term academic and career aspirations and goals.

Racial self-efficacy speaks to the belief in one's capability to read, recast, and resolve racially stressful encounters.[6] It involves believing that you can meet the demands of your racial environment and accomplish the racial tasks that may lie before you.[7] Racial self-efficacy starts with a positive self-image and a sense of self-worth fortified with inner strength. It is empowered by a mental state that has been made ready for a lifelong battle against accepting dehumanization.

Replacing and replenishing the energizing forces needed to constantly create effective resistance involves knowledge of self, racial, and ethnic identity, Black history, spirituality, and self-care. *Replace it* speaks to replenishing the spirit and is perhaps the most essential tool a resister can possess. The richness of our Black histories—the triumphs and struggles, the artistic, cultural, and political achievements of Black people throughout the diaspora—constitute elements of the cultural knowledge needed to assist Black women in assembling their resistance skills. Knowing one's own racial history, as well as the ethnic and national diasporic histories of others (African American, Caribbean, African), opens up new routes to resistance. In our work with Black college women, we urge them to embrace those reasons they came to college in the first place. In this assignment, students reconnect with their original dreams: to be the first in the family to earn a degree, to become a physician to improve health outcomes in her community, to head to law school to fight for justice. Reading many of the great books written across time by, for, and about Black people in America can help explain and sustain our liberatory consciousness. They spark our imagination and our innovation. They teach Black women to not only know from whence they came, but to also imagine an antiracist, antisexist, antihomophobic future that honors all of us fully in all of our humanity. When Black students read biographies or autobiographies of famous Black individuals throughout history, we ask them to reflect on the portraits of these ancestors, nuancing the incomplete or distorted histories of resistance that most American students had been taught. For example, Rosa Parks became the mother of the modern-day civil rights movement. Yet how many times has Rosa Parks been depicted as a tired old lady frustrated with sitting in the back of the bus, versus being described as the well-trained community organizer and civil rights activist that she actually was? And in their high school US History courses, how often was the Reverend Dr. Martin Luther King depicted solely as a nonviolent peacemaking integrationist? Why was his fervent opposition to the ravages of American capitalism and his disdain of the US role in the Vietnam War downplayed? How many students know that King's Poor People's Campaign was closely aligned with the movement begun by the Black Panther Party to self-determine and empower individuals and institutions within the Black community? How does this knowledge expand our understanding of social movements of the past? How does it inform the present and ready us for the future?

The cultural scripts we live with, the master narratives we have been taught, and the common cultural stereotypes society insists on perpetuating are designed to preserve the prevailing social order and to keep Black people subjugated. Lessons emerging from our cultural knowledge help us to interpret and challenge mainstream knowledge claims, and it is from this source that the life-sustaining counternarratives of the historically marginalized are revealed. We resist the master narratives and we create in their place new ways of knowing and being that arise from our missing, underrepresented, and previously silenced perspectives. We use our history to learn of the resisters who came before us. They laid the groundwork for future generations to build on in our ongoing battle for social justice. When we replace mistruths with the actual truths of our past, resistors see their connection to the lineage of resistance. Sister mentors and their mentees can enter into growth-promoting mentoring relationships, where together they strengthen one another's warrior spirits and further develop one another's psychological facilities and activist skills.

Rochelle had never joined a protest march. As a first-year student living away from home, this was her first time doing a lot of new things. She saw the BLM flyer posted on the wall of the student union, and she heard the other students talking about the march. It was the one-year anniversary of the death of Breanna Taylor. Her murder was on everyone's mind.[8] Groups of students gathered in the union, anxiously debating what they should do. Some students proposed a rendezvous with the planned memorial march downtown. They called it "a social action" and said it was an important way for voices to be heard. A few White students who heard the protesters scoffed and belittled their suggestions. They called the march useless, performative, and a big waste of time. But those comments seemed to make the Black students even more determined. "This matters to us!"

they shouted. "The pain hasn't gone away for us. This is our fight—and it should be yours too."

Rochelle listened intently, trying to decide what she should do. She had an exam coming up that she needed to study for. Should she spend the day at the rally and march to the statehouse, or find a study carrel in the library and hunker down with her textbooks? Her study partners warned her that if she chose the march, there would be a price to pay. They warned that the professor would hold it against her and assume she didn't care enough about passing the course. On the morning of the march, Rochelle could hear the other women in her dorm getting ready for the event. It seemed like an easy decision for them, but this was all new for Rochelle. She sat confused at the edge of her bed. *Should I stay and study? What if something happens at the march?* She had never thought about these matters before. *What happened to Breanna was wrong, and there's still no arrest of the police officers who shot her, much less a conviction. She was just minding her business with her boyfriend, and now she's dead. Could what happened to Breanna Taylor happen to me?*

Rochelle took a deep breath. She decided to call her mentor, Professor Sands, to get her opinion on what she should do. Professor Sands knew of the planned march and had herself thought about attending. She listened carefully, and asked Rochelle a few questions: Who else would be going with her? Did they have a plan for what to do if the situation got out of control? It was clear to the professor that this was important to Rochelle. She could hear her mentee trying to balance the fear she felt with the satisfaction of knowing this was the right thing for her to do. Professor Sands spoke, validating Rochelle. "This march for racial justice is important to you. You need to be there and, frankly, I do too. Do you think the members of the BSO would mind if I join you?" Smiling, Rochelle said, "I'll check, but I'm sure it'll be alright." "Great, then let's go," Professor Sands said to Rochelle. "I'll meet you in the quad. Let's get down there before dark."

Police brutality captured the attention of many American citizens as huge numbers of organized protests erupted across the nation. These events compelled so many young adults, like Rochelle, to think about their own vulnerabilities—as people of color, as women, as queer or disabled, and as members of any other historically marginalized communities. Suddenly, driving while Black, being observed with suspicion in public spaces, and becoming the victim of criminal justice wrongdoing aren't horrific misfortunes unfolding in other people's lives: they are potential tragedies knocking at your door. Rochelle made a set of important connections: this is about me, about my identity as a Black woman, about my taking a stand in the fight for social justice.

Professor Sands picked up on Rochelle's emerging sense of heightened vulnerability, her need to be proactive, and her desire to help shape a more just world. As her mentor, the professor had witnessed Rochelle's growth over the year they had been together. She knew how potent it can be when identity (*who I am*) and ideology (*what I believe*) merge full force in the life of a young adult.[9] She was moved by Rochelle's commitment to the cause and was proud of her decision to resist in this way. But there was more that motivated her choice to accompany Rochelle. Talking the talk is a whole lot easier than walking the walk. Later at the march, the crowd began to chant, "This is what democracy looks like!" Professor Sands pumped her fist in the air with the rest of the crowd, feeling confident, courageous, and grateful for this opportunity to act on her convictions. Showing up (and receiving huge applause from the students who saw her) speaks to how social action has the potential to also enrich a mentor's life. Since the march, Rochelle has made new connections with student activists on campus who similarly care about these issues and feel that this is their battle too. Professor Sands knew in her heart that her attendance was for both of them, mentor and mentee. She went to the march with Rochelle not as a White savior, but as a Sister Resister, standing in unity with others.

We end this section with the following advice. Ask the Black female students that you work with about their resistance narratives. Ask them to tell you a story of when they stood up to racism or racial bias. You may be surprised at their courage and ingenuity. You may also get a sense from their perspective of what attitudes, interpersonal dynamics, institutional policies or curricula matters need to be challenged or need to be protected. Finally, you may get a sense of how they approach resistance—what strategies they design and execute, who they turn to for help, and how they assess their effectiveness.

Mental Health and Resistance

Mental health refers to well-being across emotional, psychological, and social domains. *Well-being* is also known as *wellness*. It encompasses quality of life, and it asks: Am I living my best life? The influence of mental health on people's thoughts, actions, and feelings, while coping with the vicissitudes of life, is enormous. This connection between well-being, behaviors, and the integration of the mind, body, and spirit broadly encompasses *behavioral health*.

Resistance is a strong ally of emotional well-being. More specifically, Sister Resisters help to maintain Black college mentees' wellness and ask: What is in my mentee's best interest? *Is my mentee living her best life?* They do this by employing the resistance framework outlined in this book and unite with their mentees in setting boundaries, expecting justice, pursuing their dreams, asking for assistance, cultivating community, and naming oppression. What's not in the service of wellness and health promotion is racism, given its brutal ties to distress, addiction, and risky sexual activity.[10] Adverse childhood experiences (ACES), such as parents' divorce, poverty, intimate partner violence, and neglect, exacerbate college students' developmental vulnerability to mental health challenges. The coronavirus pandemic and its global disruption, rising racial tensions, and preexisting economic marginalization have also contributed to growing mental health fragility among many Black students. Research shows that psychological distress adversely impacts academic performance, motivation, and retention.[11] The following case study examines mental health and describes a Sister Resister shining her lamp to light her mentee's path.

Taylor is a first-generation college student in her third year. She identifies as Black. In addition to her eighteen college credits, she has a full-time job. Taylor was placed on academic probation after failing a science course and she is working hard to improve her grades. The majority of Taylor's childhood was spent in foster care. In one of her many foster families, she developed a close relationship with her foster sister, who looked out for her in their neglectful home environment. Taylor's job enables her to help her unemployed sibling, who is now a single mother of two small children. For several days last semester, Taylor left college and her unfinished lab experiments to babysit her nephews while her sister interviewed for jobs. Taylor's lab professor viewed Taylor's unexcused absences as irresponsible. Upon learning of Taylor's financial and home situation, some faculty were understanding, whereas others concluded that Taylor was not an ideal candidate for her scholarship given how "messy" her life was. Taylor panics in the presence of conflict and turns to food for comfort. Although Taylor loves chemistry, she hates the lab. Her lab mates gawk at her body. She has heard the N-word more than once and has been called *fatty*.

Ava is Taylor's academic advisor. She, too, was a first-generation college student, nearly a decade ago. Her father's job loss required Ava to exit college for a year in order to work. Over the years, Ava has chosen to educate herself about diversity. Doing so alerted her to the higher rates of Black children in foster care, disordered eating among children and adolescents with trauma histories, and racism in higher education. During her own teen years, Ava struggled with an eating disorder. To help manage her anxiety, Ava entered therapy and continues to benefit from her counselor's help.

As a Sister Resister, Ava created a brave and safe space for Taylor to talk about the multiple challenges that overwhelm her. Ava's sociopolitical awareness distinguishes her from other mentors. Like most White women, Ava was not socialized to understand the lived experiences of Taylor or her other Black female mentees. Ava's graduate training program did not prepare her to recognize and disrupt her White silence about racism or to see the White fragility that supports this silence. Ava also realizes that Taylor's cultural histories may have courted some suspicion regarding Ava's capacity to be a competent mentor. But together, they stayed the course.

While listening to Taylor tell her story about her lab experiences, Ava was saddened to hear Taylor recount the story of overt racism from her classmates, but she was not shocked. Ava detected the body policing and recognized the racial trauma when Taylor was called a racial slur by her peers who she thought were her friends. *Racial trauma* is race-based traumatic stress and is the psychological, emotional, and physical injury from experiencing real and perceived racism.[12] Ava also uncovered the White centering in faculty language when Taylor's life was referred to as "messy." *White centering* speaks to the belief, whether conscious or not, that Whiteness is "normal" and BIPOC are "other."[13] Thinking back to her college experience, Ava did not recall her family's financial situation referred to as problematic in this or in any other way. In fact, when her school learned of Ava's distress, she received financial assistance that enabled her to return to college sooner rather than later.

Ava considered what to do and what not to do. She was not going to abandon Taylor, who bravely divulged a painful racist encounter. Ava was also not going to hide behind the First Amendment to protect hateful speech. Suggesting that Taylor pursue time-intensive bureaucratic redress also would not be fair to a young woman who is clearly overworked and struggling. Moreover, the university needs to take responsibility for addressing a climate where overt racism is allowed to take hold. Ava used her resistance skills to hold the university accountable to its mission statement of antiracism. In compliance with and respect for the chain of command, Ava consulted her supervisor and informed her of the situation. Together, they advocated for additional antiracism training for staff, faculty, and students. In addition, Ava alerted Taylor's faculty that overt racist behavior was happening on campus (most likely in their programs) and in a lab that receives federal monies. Accounts of racial discrimination could make the lab vulnerable to a loss of federal aid. Ava and her supervisor encouraged the faculty to contact the lab supervisor about the event that occurred. These are actions undertaken by the women in the service of opposing racism.

Taylor and Ava share many strengths: grit, value of family, and a quest for higher education. Ava did not lose sight of Taylor's strengths, nor did she lose sight of her own strengths, which were at the forefront of her work with her mentee. One of Ava's strengths was her ability to speak truthfully. Her value of Taylor led her to validate Taylor's complex history. She said to Taylor: "Your experiences in the lab are like a mirror, showing you how negatively others view you. Please do not allow them to dictate your right to be in that lab. Also, in the future, talk to your professors if you are unable to finish your science experiments. Not doing so puts you in academic hot water."

Although it is true that many colleges have focused on improving student mental health and have hired diverse counselors across identity differences, many BIPOC students are still not receiving the mental health services that they need. Compared to White students, BIPOC students are more likely to feel overwhelmed, yet many students resist coming in for counseling.[14] Culturally informed stigma impacts mental health–seeking behavior. Being perceived as weak or crazy, as well as having limited numbers of therapists of color to work with, adversely impacts help seeking.[15] Despite this conundrum, Ava encouraged Taylor to take note of the tremendous campus resources available, which include the Counseling Center, the Disability Resource Center, and the Office for First-Generation Student Success. Ava normalized help seeking, telling Taylor that lots of students with anxiety, depression, trauma, and other health conditions can receive, by law, accommodations such as extra time on tests and different testing locations. As a Sister Resister, Ava was inspired by Taylor's dedication to her education and was able to connect with her mentee, helping her push through challenges that may well have halted her education.

Self-Care, Collaboration, and Resistance

Essential to Ava and Taylor's well-being is self-care. Audre Lorde said, "Caring for myself is not self-indulgence, it is self-preservation, and that is an act of political warfare."[16] Lorde's quote clarifies the necessity of self-care for those of us who engage in resistance work. In addition to therapy, Ava swims several times a week and practices yoga; she finds doing so has transformed her relationship with anxiety and with her eating disorder.

Self-care is sustaining to healthy cross-racial relationships. It is life affirming and it provides the energy that is needed to fight the good fight and to stay in the race. Self-care allows us to cope with disappointment, disapproval, and discouragement. In reality, the *self* in self-care is plural. Resistance work cannot be done alone because it is a call to action. To remain physically and psychologically well, recover from opposing racism, and stay optimistic when change is painfully slow, self-care is vital.

Self-care requires knowledge of and ongoing connection with allies. We depend on these nurturing, validating, and sustaining relationships for constructive criticism and for counsel. Community reminds us of who we are, our mission, and what we value. It reaffirms our capacity to engage in relationships that are not always easy, and it fortifies our commitment to people who hold our resistance work in high esteem.

To open doors that resist opening and to coexist with people who resist change, Sister Resisters must have access to caring, supportive, and nurturing communities.

Staring down systems that view justice as divisive will at times require mentors to seek out their own mentors and/or therapists. Sometimes help is needed to discern which issues we need to go to the mat for and which battles we can afford to defer. Acknowledging when we need to rest our bodies, seek professional help, depart for the quiet and silence to meditate, practice mindfulness and prayer, move our bodies, and feed ourselves with nutritious food allows us to be and stay well.

Sister Resistance struggle is real and insists on self-care, compassion, and respect for the difficult yet beautiful work that we are engaged in daily. Fatigue will set in. For this reason, regularly grabbing a bag of chips and an energy drink cannot fuel us for long-term endurance. We also would not send our children, beloved partners, and dear friends off to battle with such inadequate nutrition. Self-care is self-respect and self-love.

An essential self-care tool in resistance work is anticipation of pushback. Sister Resisters are mindful of the dogged reticence to embrace a position of justice that is contrary to someone else's perspective on race. Sociopolitical awareness of others' rebuke and denigration of antiracism work is intimidating but integral to sustainability in justice-focused endeavors. Sister Resisters must face the difficult reality that there are people, even within our inner circles and immediate families, who neither share nor applaud our vision of inclusion. Wellness honors that when we commit to growth, there will be losses amid substantial gains. While some changes will be welcomed, others will not. They will hurt and feel like what they are—a loss.

We respect that relational change can feel intimidating. The brilliant news is that this work, of growing mindfulness and severing our tethers to inequity, will develop the self and encourage critical reflection. Ask: Where in my body do I feel stress when discussing racism? What makes me frightened to speak my truth? On whom can I rely to support me in my antiracism work? What helps me to enter into a state of calmness and peace? Do I rely heavily on substances, including nicotine, caffeine, and alcohol, to relax in my antiracism work? If so, why? These questions help to assess the care of the self. We burn out when we do not invest in the health of our body, mind, and spirit. Honor the resistance work and what it takes to be successful. Be brave enough to start this journey and love yourself enough to carry it through. Our struggles develop our strengths, and our strengths are multiplied when we embrace this work together.

Conclusion

Becoming an antiracist White ally to Black college women is life alter-ing, for both the mentor and the mentee. Detecting, naming, opposing, and replacing racism are unnatural acts for White women. Providing emotional support to others who may be struggling is part of being a Sister Resister. We are awake to and humbled by the enormity of our ask. And still, we invite White women to move into this uncharted ter-ritory and to stay put. Doing so is not always easy; it requires humility and honesty. And to stay motivated through the hard times (and there will definitely be hard times), determination and commitment are key. We affirm hope and liberation, born from communion with others united in a shared vision. Measured by each conversation from an inten-tional mentor, Sister Resisters harness their power and knowledge for good. They demand that higher education live up to its lofty creed, to uplift and educate all who enter. A word of encouragement to stay the course can lighten the load carried by our young Black mentees and help them hold fast to their dreams.

Now is the time for intentional and deliberate action. As Sister Resisters, united together in relationship, vulnerability, trust, and healthy interdependence, we journey forward as one. We invite you into this sisterhood of good trouble as we honor the lives we touch and, in the words of Layla Saad, become the best ancestors we can be. As our mothers would say, "Right is right, and right don't wrong nobody." Welcome.

Afterword

A S BLACK FEMALE PROFESSORS and researchers in higher education, we acknowledge that we coexist within multiple contradictions. For example, we implore young women to enter college as a means of achieving the personal, economic, and occupational success that is the prelude to social mobility, yet we see these same Black women experience subtle and overt racism on our campuses, and college completion rates reflect distressing racial disparities. Moreover, we find that when and if Black women complete their education, too often they're left mired in high college tuition debt.

We are witness to an undeniable under-representation of Black students, staff, and faculty on most university campuses. As a result, when our Black students find themselves overwhelmed by their circumstances, there are few employed Black people who understand the stressors that Black women face. For this and many other reasons, we fully endorse the hiring of additional Black faculty, administrators, and staff. Their presence is additive—not only for BIPOC students, but for all students across our college and university campuses. The urgency of this call is not new, nor unfortunately is our disappointment that hiring trends continue to stagnate, particularly in regard to the employment of full-time Black faculty.

While we wait for colleges and universities to live up to the principles proclaimed in their diversity, equity, and inclusion mission statements, the work of bolstering the success of Black college women must not languish. We wrote this book in an effort to highlight the challenges faced by many Black students in predominantly White institutions and to provide a framework for thinking about these challenges.

The competent and confident use of critical skills to support Black students' educational journeys is the destination.

When this book went to press, we were emerging from a fourteen-month-long pandemic lockdown. Many undergraduate and graduate students across the country had been shifted from their classrooms to remote learning as campuses were shuttered. Student supports were moved online in a reduced capacity or in some places were not offered at all. The pandemic taught us just how important it is to keep our students' needs at the forefront of what we do. This is particularly important for those students who are chronically battered by racial and economic forces that are weathering to mind and body.

What we have learned about resistance rooted in Black people's struggles and triumphs has given birth to our Sister Resister model. In addition, we both have enduring relationships with White women who we think of as Sister Resisters. These relationships have been inspirational and have enabled us to trust that our resistance framework is attainable. The relational ties that we have forged over the years, and some cases decades, distinguish Sister Resisters from other White women, whose lives are void of these powerful connections. It has been our experience that strong cross-racial alliances foster vulnerability and trust, and it is in these connections that women share the requisite knowledge to detect, name, and oppose racism. These alliances have illuminated the ways in which racism and sexism have manifested in all of our lives, across institutional domains, and over time. The work of resistance beckons us all.

Preparing for Sister Resistance

Even experienced Sister Resisters need help analyzing, identifying, and strategizing how best to be effective with students and colleagues. Often, a multipronged resistance approach is needed to address inequities on multiple levels, including personal, interpersonal, and structural. The following strategies are a guide to Sister Resistance:

- Partner with Black college women to name and navigate gendered and racial oppression within predominantly White higher education environments.
- Join with mentees to build and stock up on a repertoire of resistance strategies.
- Realize that the work of resistance is difficult and that shifts in existing relationships may occur.
- Accept that there are people who will neither understand nor condone your Sister Resistance.
- Be willing to broach race with your mentee; develop the ability to speak about race with others as well.
- Resist racial silence.
- Educate yourself about Black women's history.
- Educate yourself about the multiple and varied cultures of Black women on campus.
- Adopt an assets-based model in your work with Black women.
- Educate yourself about the culturally based strengths that have enabled Black women to love, live well, and overcome oppression.
- Call out institutional racism on your campus.
- Identify the ways in which White supremacy has influenced your personal development, coping capacities, notions of normalcy, and your own career trajectory.

- Know how to analyze, apply, and assess your work with Black women in ways that acknowledge and appreciate intersectional dynamics.
- Practice cultural humility; honor the fact that learning and unlearning are ongoing processes.
- Gain clarity about who you can and cannot count on for resistance support.
- Maintain relationships with BIPOC to strengthen critical consciousness and accountability to others.
- Pay attention and remain open to constructive feedback. Be teachable.
- Cultivate a community of Sister Resisters. We all need each other's support!

NOTES

PREFACE

1. This quote has been attributed to the great blues musician B. B. King, but many African Americans, like ourselves, grew up with these or similar words ringing in our ears.

2. Bill Hussar, Jijun Zhang, Sarah Hein, Ke Wang, Ashley Roberts, Jiashan Cui, Mary Smith, Farrah Bullock Mann, Amy Barmer, and Rita Dilig, "College Enrollment Rates," in *The Condition of Education, 2020* (Washington, DC: National Center for Education Statistics, 2020), 124–126, https://nces.ed.gov/programs/coe /pd. The NCES data suggests that there was no measurable difference in the college enrollment data for Black people who were also female between 2000 and 2018.

3. Dimpal Jain and Gloria Crisp, "Creating Inclusive and Equitable Environments for Racially Minoritized Learners: Recommendations for Research, Policy and Practice," ASHE-NITE Paper Series, 2018, https://nite-education.org/wp -content/uploads/2020/02/Creating-Inclusive-and-Equitable-environments -for-racially-minoritized-adult-learners-FINAL.pdf

4. The report states, "Students at for-profits are disproportionately older, African American, and female, and are more likely to be single parents." Center for Analysis of Postsecondary Education and Employment, "For-Profit Colleges: By the Numbers," CAPSEE, February 2018, https://capseecenter.org/research/by -the-numbers/for-profit-college-infographic/.

5. Tressie McMillan Cottom, *Lower Ed: The Troubling Rise of For-Profit Colleges in the New Economy* (New York: New Press, 2017). Another article states, "Student loan debt in the U.S. is currently at a back-breaking $1.56 trillion from over 44 million borrowers according to Forbes. Over $929 billion of that debt is shouldered by women, and according to a report by the American Association of University Women, Black women carry two-thirds more debt than their white counterparts." BET Staff, "For-Profit Schools Target the Black Community. Here's How You Can Avoid the Scam," BET, September 18, 2019, https:// www.bet.com/news/national/2019/09/18/for-profit-schools-target-the-black -community--heres-how-you-can.html.

6. See also Ariel Gelrud Shiro and Richard V. Reeves, "The For-Profit College System Is Broken and the Biden Administration Needs to Fix It," Brookings, January 12, 2021, https://www.brookings.edu/blog/how-we-rise/2021/01/12/

the-for-profit-college-system-is-broken-and-the-biden-administration-needs
-to-fix-it/.

7. Some of these books include, among others, Lori D. Patton and Natasha N. Croom, eds., *Critical Perspectives on Black Women and College Success* (New York: Routledge, 2017); Rachelle Winkle-Wagner, *The Unchosen Me: Race, Gender, and Identity Among Black Women in College* (Baltimore: Johns Hopkins University Press, 2009); Felecia Commodore, Dominique J. Baker, and Andrew T. Arroyo, *Black Women College Students: A Guide to Student Success in Higher Education* (New York: Routledge, 2018); and Elizabeth Aries, *Race and Class Matters at an Elite College* (Philadelphia: Temple University Press, 2008).

8. Juan F. Carrillo, Danielle Parker Moore, and Timothy Condor, *Mentoring Students of Color: Naming the Politics of Race, Social Class, Gender, and Power* (Leiden: Brill, 2019); Torie Weiston-Serdan, *Critical Mentoring: A Practical Guide* (Sterling, VA: Stylus Publishing, 2017); Susanne Tedrick, *Women of Color in Tech: A Blueprint for Inspiring and Mentoring the Next Generation of Technology Innovators* (Indianapolis: Wiley, 2020).

9. Tracy Robinson and Janie Victoria Ward, "'A Belief in Self Far Greater than Anyone's Disbelief': Cultivating Resistance Among African American Female Adolescents," *Women & Therapy* 11, no. 3–4 (1991): 87–103.

10. Racial battle fatigue (RBF) was a term coined by critical race theorist William Smith. RBF is described as the physical and psychological toll suffered due to constant and unceasing discrimination, microaggressions, and stereotype threat. See Kenneth Fashing-Varner, Katrice A. Albert, Roland W. Mitchell, and Chaunda M. Allen, *Racial Battle Fatigue in Higher Education: Exposing the Myth of Post-Racial America* (Lanham, MD: Rowman & Littlefield, 2015). See also William A. Smith, Jalil Bishop Mustaffa, Chantal M. Jones, Tommy J. Curry, and Walter R. Allen, "'You Make Me Wanna Holler and Throw up Both My Hands!': Campus Culture, Black Misandric Microaggressions, and Racial Battle Fatigue," *International Journal of Qualitative Studies in Education* 29, no. 9 (2016): 1189–1209.

11. See Gwendolyn Midlo Hall and Pero G. Dagbovie, *Haunted by Slavery: A Memoir of a Southern White Woman in the Freedom Struggle* (Chicago: Haymarket Books, 2021); Cynthia Stokes Brown, *Refusing Racism: White Allies and the Struggle for Civil Rights* (New York: Teachers College Press, 2002); David L. Chappell, *Inside Agitators: White Southerners in the Civil Rights Movement* (Baltimore: Johns Hopkins University Press, 1996).

12. Kristen Mack and John Palfrey, "Capitalizing Black and White: Grammatical Justice and Equity," MacArthur Foundation, August 26, 2020, https://www.macfound.org/press/perspectives/capitalizing-black-and-white-grammatical-justice-and-equity.

13. American Psychological Association Divisions 16 and 44, *Key Terms and Concepts in Understanding Gender Diversity and Sexual Orientation among Students* (Washington, DC: American Psychological Association, 2015), https://www.apa.org/pi/lgbt/programs/safe-supportive/lgbt/key-terms.pdf.

14. Misty M. Ginicola, Cheri Smith, and Joel M. Filmore, eds, *Affirmative Counseling with LGBTQI+ People* (Alexandria, VA: American Counseling Association, 2017).
15. Ginicola, Smith, and Filmore, *Affirmative Counseling with LGBTQI+ People.*
16. American Psychological Association Divisions 16 and 44, "Key Terms and Concepts"; American Psychological Association, "APA Style Grammar Guidelines: Bias Free Language/Gender," APA Style, September 2019, https://apastyle .apa.org/style-grammar-guidelines/bias-free-language/gender?_ga =2.216202262.1637997154.1621531316-1630257714.1617762335.
17. Ibram X. Kendi, *How to Be an Antiracist* (New York: One World, 2019).
18. Charles M. Blow, "We Need a Second Great Migration," *Sun Sentinel*, January 8, 2021, https://www.sun-sentinel.com/featured/sns-nyt-op-second-great -migration-20210108-ke6ucmzo4fc5thw4pdeme3cnj4-story.html.

INTRODUCTION

1. Robin DiAngelo, *White Fragility: Why It's So Hard for White People to Talk about Racism* (Boston: Beacon Press, 2018), 94.
2. Jean Baker Miller, *Toward a New Psychology of Women* (Boston: Beacon Press, 1987).
3. DiAngelo, *White Fragility*, 62.
4. Patricia Hill Collins, *Black Feminist Thought: Knowledge, Consciousness, and the Politics of Empowerment*, 2nd ed. (New York: Routledge, 2000).
5. Camara Phyllis Jones, "Levels of Racism: A Theoretic Framework and a Gardener's Tale," *American Journal of Public Health* 90, no. 8 (2000): 1212; Vann R. Newkirk II, "Trump's EPA Concludes Environmental Racism Is Real," *The Atlantic*, February 28, 2018, https://www.theatlantic.com/politics/archive/2018/02/ the-trump-administration-finds-that-environmental-racism-is-real/554315/.
6. Akasha Gloria Hull, *Soul Talk: The New Spirituality of African American Women* (Rochester, VT: Inner Traditions, 2001); Ruth Frankenberg, *White Women, Race Matters: The Social Construction of Whiteness* (London: Routledge, 1993); Joy James, *Seeking the Beloved Community: A Feminist Race Reader* (New York: State University of New York Press, 2014).
7. We use here the definition of intersectionality introduced by Grzanka, Santos, and Moradi (2017). They see it as "the study and critique of how multiple social systems intersect to produce and sustain complex inequalities" (453). Patrick R. Grzanka, Kristen A. Gonzalez, and Lisa B. Spanierman, "White Supremacy and Counseling Psychology: A Critical-Conceptual Framework," *Counseling Psychologist* 47, no. 4 (2019): 478–529.
8. Some of the foundational texts exploring Black feminism and womanism theory include Alice Walker, *In Search of Our Mother's Gardens: Womanist Prose* (London: Phoenix, 1983); Katie G. Cannon, *Katie's Canon: Womanism and the Soul of the Black Community* (New York: Continuum, 1998); Combahee River Collective, "Combahee River Collective Statement," in *Home Girls: A Black Feminist Anthology*, edited by Barbara Smith (New Brunswick: Rutgers University

Press, 2000), 264–274; Collins, *Black Feminist Thought*, 2nd ed.; and Deborah K. King, "Multiple Jeopardy, Multiple Consciousness: The Context of a Black Feminist Ideology," *Signs* 14, no. 1 (1988): 42–72. Our discussions of critical race feminism in education are informed by Venus Evans-Winters and Jennifer Esposito, "Other People's Daughters: Critical Race Feminism and Black Girls' Education," *Educational Foundations*, 24, no. 1–2 (2010): 11–24. And for more on critical race feminism, see Adrien Katherine Wing, ed., *Critical Race Feminism: A Reader*, 2nd ed. (New York: NYU Press, 2003). Finally, our discussions of power, privilege, and intersectionality are informed by the theories of Patricia Hill Collins and Sirma Bilge, *Intersectionality*, 2nd ed. (Cambridge: Polity Press, 2020); and Kimberlé Crenshaw, "Demarginalizing the Intersection of Race and Sex: A Black Feminist Critique of Antidiscrimination Doctrine, Feminist Theory and Antiracist Politics," *University of Chicago Legal Forum* 1, no. 8 (1989): 139–168. The concept of intersectionality predates Crenshaw and other modern Black feminists, with intellectual antecedents that include Anna Julia Cooper's book *A Voice from the South* (1892), which offered an intersectional analysis that took into account race, class, gender, and global perspectives on social inequality; and Ida B. Wells (*A Red Record*, 1895), whose reporting on lynching pointed out how sexuality, racism, and sexism were intertwined. Later Black feminists such as Angela Davis, Deborah King, Patricia Hill Collins, and others expanded the theory in the twentieth century.

9. Andrea J. Ritchie and Monique W. Morris, *Centering Black Women, Girls, Gender Nonconforming People and Fem(me)s in Campaigns for Expanded Sanctuary and Freedom Cities* (Atlanta: National Black Women's Policy Institute, 2017).

10. Stephen Vassallo, *Critical Educational Psychology* (Baltimore: Johns Hopkins University Press, 2017), 120–121.

11. Michael Nakkula and Eric Toshalis, *Understanding Youth: Adolescent Development for Educators* (Cambridge, MA: Harvard Education Press, 2006).

12. Tracy Robinson and Janie Victoria Ward, "'A Belief in Self Far Greater than Anyone's Disbelief': Cultivating Healthy Resistance among African American Female Adolescents," in *Women, Girls, and Psychotherapy: Reframing Resistance*, edited by C. Gilligan et al. (New York: Haworth Press, 1991) 87–103; Agnes Martin, Noreen Boadi, Caroline Fernandes, Sherry Watt, and Tracy Robinson-Wood, "Applying Resistance Theory to Depression in Black Women," *Journal of Systemic Therapies* 32, no. 1 (2013): 1–13; Tracy Robinson-Wood, "Measuring Resistance in Black Women: The Resistance Modality Inventory," *Journal of Systemic Therapies* 33, no. 2 (2014): 62–77; Janie Victoria Ward, "Uncovering Truths, Recovering Lives," in *Urban Girls Revisited: Building Strengths*, edited by Bonnie Leadbeater and Niobe Way (New York: NYU Press: 2007), 243–260; Janie Victoria Ward, *The Skin We're In: Teaching Our Children to Be Emotionally Strong, Socially Smart, Spiritually Connected* (New York: Fireside, 2000). See also Tracy Robinson-Wood, Oyenike Balogun-Mwangi, Amanda Weber, Elda Zeko-Underwood, Shelly-Ann Collins-Rawle, Ami Popat-Jain, Atsushi Matsumoto, and Elizabeth Cook, "'What Is It Going to Be Like?' A

Phenomenological Investigation of Racial, Gendered and Sexual Microaggressions among Highly Educated Individuals," *Journal of Qualitative Psychology* 7, no. 1 (2020): 43–58.

13. Tara J. Yosso, "Whose Culture Has Capital? A Critical Race Theory Discussion of Community Cultural Wealth," *Race Ethnicity and Education* 8, no. 1 (March 2005): 69–91.

14. Collins, *Black Feminist Thought*, 2nd ed.; Katie Geneva Cannon, *Womanism and the Soul of the Black Community* (New York: Continuum, 1998); Katie Geneva Cannon, "Remembering What We Never Knew," *Journal of Women and Religion* 16 (1998):167–177.

15. See also Kesho Scott, *The Habit of Surviving: Black Women's Strategies for Life* (New Brunswick: Rutgers University Press, 1991).

16. Frankenberg, *White Women, Race Matters*, 167. See also Kim A. Case, "Discovering the Privilege of Whiteness: White Women's Reflections on Anti-racist Identity and Ally Behavior," *Journal of Social Issues* 68, no. 1 (2012): 78–96. For an example of a White woman at the forefront of antiracist activism whose resistance persisted in the face of death threats and social ostracism, see Mab Segrest, *My Mama's Dead Squirrel: Lesbian Essays on Southern Culture* (Ithaca, NY: Firebrand Books, 1985); and Segrest's memoir, *Memoir of a Race Traitor: Fighting Racism in the American South* (New York: New Press, 2019). Two other White women activists of note are Elly Bulkin and Minnie Bruce Pratt. Bulkin is a Jewish feminist activist whose establishment of deep conversations among Black, White, and Jewish women in long-term sustained relationships about race, class, and religion lead to the creation of the journal *Bridges*. Inspired by the Combahee River Collective, Bulkin's work was intersectional before such work became popular. Pratt was a Southern lesbian woman who lost her children when she revealed her sexual orientation. This event led her to engage in bridge work, connecting the homophobic power of the state to remove children from families to the power of the state to uphold racism and other forms of oppression.

17. Maya Angelou, *Letter to My Daughter* (New York: Random House, 2009).

18. Carole Widick, Clyde A. Parker, and Lee Knefelkamp, "Erik Erikson and Psychosocial Development," *New Directions for Student Services*, no. 4 (1978): 1–17. See also Marcia Baxter Magolda, "The Activity of Meaning Making: A Holistic Perspective on College Student Development," *Journal of College Student Development* 50, no. 6 (2009): 621–639.

19. Shirley M. Clark and Mary Corcoran, "Perspectives on the Professional Socialization of Women Faculty," *Journal of Higher Education* 57, no. 1 (1986): 20–43.

20. Torie Weiston-Serdan, *Critical Mentoring: A Practical Guide* (Sterling, VA: Stylus Publishing, 2016).

21. Ward, *The Skin We're In*.

22. See Vargas et al.'s reframing of mentorship training using critical race theory. Jose H. Vargas, Carrie L. Saetermoe, and Gabriela Chavira, "Using Critical Race Theory to Reframe Mentor Training: Theoretical Considerations Regarding

the Ecological Systems of Mentorship," *Higher Education* 81, no. 5 (May 2021): 1043–1062.

23. David A. Thomas, "Racial Dynamics in Cross-Race Developmental Relationships," *Administrative Science Quarterly* 38, no. 2 (1993): 169-194.

24. Deidre M. Anglin and Jay C. Wade, "Racial Socialization, Racial Identity, and Black Students' Adjustment to College," *Cultural Diversity and Ethnic Minority Psychology* 13, no. 3 (2007): 207-215. See also Patricia C. Thompson, Louis P. Anderson, and Roger A. Bakeman, "Effects of Racial Socialization and Racial Identity on Acculturative Stress in African American College Students," *Cultural Diversity and Ethnic Minority Psychology* 6, no. 2 (2000): 196-210.

25. Janet E. Helms, "An Update of Helms's White and People of Color Racial Identity Models," in *Handbook of Multicultural Counseling*, edited by Joseph G. Ponterotto, J. Manuel Casas, Lisa A. Suzuki, and Charlene Alexander (Thousand Oaks, CA: Sage, 1995), 181-198; Thompson, Anderson, and Bakeman, "Effects of Racial Socialization"; and Elizabeth E. Parks, Robert T. Carter, and George V. Gushue, "At the Crossroads: Racial and Womanist Identity Development in Black and White Women," *Journal of Counseling and Development* 74 (1996): 624-631.

CHAPTER 1

1. Yolanda Suarez-Balcazar, Lucia Orellana-Damacela, Nelson Portillo, Jean M. Rowan, and Chelsea Andrews-Guillen, "Experiences of Differential Treatment Among College Students of Color," *Journal of Higher Education* 74, no. 4 (2003): 428-444.

2. Tracy Robinson-Wood, Oyeŋike Balogun-Mwangi, Caroline Fernandes, Ami Popat-Jain, Noreen Boadi, Atsushi Matsumoto, and Xiaolu Zhang, "Worse than Blatant Racism: A Phenomenological Investigation of Microaggressions Among Black Women," *Journal of Ethnographic & Qualitative Research* 9, no. 3 (2015): 221-236.

3. The stories we share emerge from two primary sources. Most are anonymized stories from students, faculty members and staff that we have known and worked with over the years. We heard some of these narratives in private conversations on and off campus. Other stories were voiced in formal and informal focus groups organized by the authors or by graduate students working with us. A few of the stories are fictionalized accounts, drawn from circumstances described by others in the research literature, or they represent particular matters that we have been made aware of. In general, the quotes that appear in the fictionalized accounts illustrate the thoughts and concerns we have heard Black college students express in our many decades of teaching. In the case of formal and informal focus group participants, we have edited their comments for clarity and readability in ways that protect the identity of the speaker(s).

4. Erica M. Morales, "Intersectional Impact: Black Students and Race, Gender and Class Microaggressions in Higher Education," *Race, Gender & Class* 21, no. 3–4 (2014): 48–66.

5. Chester Pierce, "Offensive Mechanisms," in *The Black Seventies*, edited by Floyd B. Barbour (Boston: Porter Sargent, 1970), 265–282; Derald Wing Sue, Christina M. Capodilupo, Gina C. Torino, Jennifer M. Bucceri, Aisha Holder, Kevin L. Nadal, and Marta Esquilin, "Racial Microaggressions in Everyday Life: Implications for Clinical Practice," *American Psychologist* 62, no. 4 (2007): 271.

6. Daniel Solorzano, Miguel Ceja, and Tara Yosso, "Critical Race Theory, Racial Microaggressions, and Campus Racial Climate: The Experiences of African American College Students," *Journal of Negro Education* 69, no. 1–2 (2000): 60–73.

7. Robinson-Wood et al., "Worse than Blatant Racism."

8. Felecia Commodore, Dominique J. Baker, and Andrew T. Arroyo, *Black Women College Students: A Guide to Student Success in Higher Education* (New York: Routledge 2018);

9. Paula J. Caplan and Jordan C. Ford, "The Voices of Diversity: What Students of Diverse Races/Ethnicities and Both Sexes Tell Us About their College Experiences and Their Perceptions about Their Institutions' Progress Toward Diversity," *Aporia* 6, no. 4 (2014): 30–69.

10. Monnica T. Williams, Isha W. Metzger, Chris Leins, and Celenia DeLapp, "Assessing Racial Trauma within a DSM-5 Framework: The UConn Racial/Ethnic Stress & Trauma Survey," *Practice Innovations* 3, no. 4 (2018): 242–260.

11. For in-depth discussions of Black students' experiences on college campuses, see Bridget Turner Kelly, Paige J. Gardner, Joakina Stone, Ashley Hixson, and Di-Tu Dissassa, "Hidden in Plain Sight: Uncovering the Emotional Labor of Black Women Students at Historically White Colleges and Universities," *Journal of Diversity in Higher Education* 14, no. 2 (2019): 203–216; Stacy A. Harwood, Margaret Browne Huntt, Ruby Mendenhall, and Jioni A. Lewis, "Racial Microaggressions in the Residence Halls: Experiences of Students of Color at a Predominantly White University," *Journal of Diversity in Higher Education* 5, no. 3 (2012): 159–173; Sylvia Hurtado, Alma R. Clayton-Pedersen, Walter Recharde Allen, and Jeffrey F. Milem, "Enhancing Campus Climates for Racial/Ethnic Diversity: Educational Policy and Practice," *Review of Higher Education* 21, no. 3 (1998): 279–302; Runi B. Mukherji, Lorenz S. Neuwirth, and Laura Limonic, "Making the Case for Real Diversity: Redefining Underrepresented Minority Students in Public Universities," *SAGE Open* 7, no. 2 (2017), https://doi.org/10.1177/2158244017707796; Julie J. Park, Nida Denson, and Nicholas A. Bowman, "Does Socioeconomic Diversity Make a Difference? Examining the Effects of Racial and Socioeconomic Diversity on the Campus Climate for Diversity," *American Educational Research Journal* 50, no. 3 (2013): 466–496.

12. Suarez-Balcazar et al., "Experiences of Differential Treatment"; Jeffrey F. Milem, Mitchell J. Chang, and Anthony Lising Antonio, *Making Diversity Work*

on Campus: A Research-Based Perspective (Washington, DC: Association of American Colleges and Universities, 2005).

13. Audre Lorde, *I Am Your Sister: Black Women Organizing across Sexualities* (New York: Kitchen Table: Women of Color Press, 1985), 4.

14. Rose M. Brewer, "Black Feminism and Womanism," in *Companion to Feminist Studies*, edited by Nancy A. Naples (Hoboken, NJ: Wiley, 2020), 91–104. Brewer argues that early twentieth-century Black suffragettes repeatedly called attention to issues of race in the early decades of the twentieth century. She wrote, "Given white middle class women's preoccupation with gender and their seeming inability to come to terms with race, 'problematic' is a way to explain Black women's historic relationship to white American feminism" (75). Deborah King argues, "The modifier 'multiple' refers not only to several, simultaneous oppressions but to the multiplicative relationships among them as well. In other words, the equivalent formulation is racism multiplied by sexism multiplied by classism." Deborah K. King, "Multiple Jeopardy, Multiple Consciousness: The Context of a Black Feminist Ideology," *Signs* 14, no. 1 (1988): 42–72, 47.

15. Robert M. Sellers, Mia A. Smith, J. Nicole Shelton, Stephanie A. J. Rowley, and Tabbye M. Chavous, "Multidimensional Model of Racial Identity: A Reconceptualization of African American Racial Identity," *Personality and Social Psychology Review* 2, no. 1 (1998): 18–39; Subrina J. Robinson, Elena Esquibel, and Marc D. Rich, "'I'm Still Here': Black Female Undergraduates' Self-Definition Narratives," *World Journal of Education* 3, no. 5 (2013): 57–71. For an in-depth discussion of how Black women and girls' development has been conceptualized in developmental science, see C. A. Agger et al, "Taking a Critical Look at Adolescent Research on Black Girls and Women: A Systematic Review" (unpublished manuscript, under review).

16. Richard L. Allen and Richard P. Bagozzi, "Consequences of the Black Sense of Self," *Journal of Black Psychology* 27, no. 1 (2001): 3–28.

17. APA Task Force on Resilience and Strength in Black Children and Adolescents, *Resilience in African American Children and Adolescents: A Vision for Optimal Development* (Washington, DC: APA, 2008), https://www.apa.org/pi/families/resources/resiliencerpt.pdf. See also the strengths and coping model for Black youth, presented in G. Nicolas, J. E. Helms, M. M. Jernigan, T. Sass, A. Skrzypek, and A. M. DeSilva, "A Conceptual Framework for Understanding the Strengths of Black Youths," *Journal of Black Psychology* 34, no. 3 (2008): 261–280. The authors argue that their model "uses resistance rather than resilience to describe healthy functioning of Black youths, because the concept of resistance incorporates the principle of active involvement of youths in changing oppressive environments rather than being shaped or debilitated by them" (264).

18. Janie Victoria Ward, "'Eyes in the Back of Your Head': Moral Themes in African American Narratives of Racial Conflict," *Journal of Moral Education* 20, no. 3 (1991): 267–281.

19. Elizabeth E. Parks, Robert T. Carter, and George V. Gushue, "At the Crossroads: Racial and Womanist Identity Development in Black and White Women," *Journal of Counseling & Development* 74, no. 6 (1996): 624–631; Christine R. Hannon, Marianne Woodside, Brittany L. Pollard, and Jorge Roman, "The Meaning of African American College Women's Experiences Attending a Predominantly White Institution: A Phenomenological Study," *Journal of College Student Development* 57, no. 6 (2016): 652–666.

20. Janie Victoria Ward, "Staying Woke," in *The Crisis of Connection: Roots, Consequences, and Solutions,* edited by Niobe Way, Alisha Ali, Carol Gilligan, and Pedro Noguera (New York: New York University Press, 2018), 106–128.

21. Michelle Wallace, *Black Macho and the Myth of the Superwoman* (London: Verso, 2015), first published in 1978; Tamara Beauboeuf-Lafontant, *Behind the Mask of the Strong Black Woman: Voice and the Embodiment of a Costly Performance* (Philadelphia: Temple University Press, 2009).

22. Cheryl L. Woods-Giscombé, "Superwoman Schema: African American Women's Views on Stress, Strength, and Health," *Qualitative Health Research* 20, no. 5 (2010): 668–683; Jasmine A. Abrams, Ashley Hill, and Morgan Maxwell, "Underneath the Mask of the Strong Black Woman Schema: Disentangling Influences of Strength and Self-Silencing on Depressive Symptoms among US Black Women," *Sex Roles* 80, no. 9 (2019): 517–526.

23. Patricia Hill Collins, *Black Feminist Thought: Knowledge, Consciousness, and the Politics of Empowerment,* 2nd ed. (New York: Routledge, 2000); Audre Lorde, *Sister Outsider: Essays and Speeches* (Berkeley: Crossing Press, 1984); June Jordan, *On Call: Political Essays* (London: Pluto, 1986)

24. Nicola A. Corbin, William A. Smith, and J. Roberto Garcia, "Trapped between Justified Anger and Being the Strong Black Woman: Black College Women Coping with Racial Battle Fatigue at Historically and Predominantly White Institutions," *International Journal of Qualitative Studies in Education* 31, no. 7 (2018): 626–643.

25. Olivia N. Perlow, "Gettin' Free: Anger as Resistance to White Supremacy within and beyond the Academy," in *Black Women's Liberatory Pedagogies,* edited by Olivia N. Perlow, Durene I. Wheeler, Sharon L. Bethea, and BarBara M. Scott (Cham: Palgrave Macmillan, 2018), 101–123. Perlow, in citing Janet Mock, argues that the "angry Black woman" stereotype dehumanizes Black women by reducing all of our individuality and complexity to a single emotion: anger. It is an erasure of the multiplicity of our identities, our histories, our cultures, our experiences, and it ultimately "shrinks us to shells of ourselves" (108).

26. Scott Seider and Daren Graves, *Schooling for Critical Consciousness: Engaging Black and Latinx Youth in Analyzing, Navigating, and Challenging Racial Injustice* (Cambridge, MA: Harvard Education Press, 2020). See also Paulo Freire, *Pedagogy of the Oppressed* (New York: Seabury Press, 1970).

27. Seider and Graves link critical consciousness in Black and Latinx youth to civic and political activism and the broader collective struggle for social justice. Seider and Graves, *Schooling for Critical Consciousness.*

28. The womanism phrase "Mama, I'm walking to Canada and I'm taking you and a bunch of other slaves with me" appears in Alice Walker, *In Search of Our Mother's Gardens: Womanist Prose* (Orlando: Harcourt Brace Jovanovich, 1983). See also Pamela Ayo Yetunde, "Black Lesbians to the Rescue! A Brief Correction with Implications for Womanist Christian Theology and Womanist Buddhology," *Religions* 8 (2017): 175.

29. Janie Victoria Ward, *The Skin We're In: Teaching Our Children to Be Emotionally Strong, Socially Smart, Spiritually Connected* (New York: Fireside, 2002).

30. Tracy Robinson and Janie Victoria Ward, "'A Belief in Self Far Greater than Anyone's Disbelief': Cultivating Resistance among African American Female Adolescents," *Women & Therapy* 11, no. 3–4 (1991): 87–103.

31. Agnes Martin, Noreen Boadi, Caroline Fernandes, Sherry Watt, and Tracy Robinson-Wood, "Applying Resistance Theory to Depression in Black Women," *Journal of Systemic Therapies* 32, no. 1 (2013): 1–13.

CHAPTER 2

1. We refer here to the oft-cited "Ain't I a Woman" speech; words that were attributed to Sojourner Truth, but were, according to historians, invented and distorted into a southern dialect for public consumption many years after Truth delivered her speech. See Nell Irvin Painter, *Sojourner Truth: A Life, a Symbol* (W. W. Norton: New York, 1997).

2. Audre Lorde, *Sister Outsider: Essays and Speeches* (Berkeley: Crossing Press, 1984), 131.

3. Cosette M. Grant, "Advancing Our Legacy: A Black Feminist Perspective on the Significance of Mentoring for African-American Women in Educational Leadership," *International Journal of Qualitative Studies in Education* 25, no. 1 (2012): 101–117. Grant discusses the importance of "prioritized mentoring" for Black female students, which places the responsibility for mentoring on White faculty and non-Black faculty, as well as on Black faculty.

4. We are using DiAngelo's definition of Whiteness, which she conceptualizes as "a constellation of processes and practices rather than as a discreet entity (i.e., skin color alone). Whiteness is dynamic, relational, and operating at all times and on myriad levels." Robin DiAngelo, "White Fragility," *International Journal of Critical Pedagogy* 3, no. 3 (2011): 54–70, 56, https://libjournal.uncg.edu/ijcp/article/view/249. DiAngelo's work builds on theories of Whiteness first articulated by African American scholars across the eighteenth, nineteenth, and twentieth centuries, including Frederick Douglass, W. E. B. DuBois, Anna Julia Cooper, James Baldwin, Toni Morrison, and many others.

5. Kim A. Case, "Discovering the Privilege of Whiteness: White Women's Reflections on Anti-Racist Identity and Ally Behavior," *Journal of Social Issues* 68, no. 1 (2012): 78–96.

6. Naomi W. Nishi, Cheryl E. Matias, Roberto Montoya, and Geneva L. Sarcedo, "Whiteness FAQ: Responses and Tools for Confronting College Classroom

Questions," *Journal of Critical Thought and Praxis* 5, no. 1 (2016): 1–36. Nishi et al. remind us that People of Color sometimes perpetuate Whiteness because they too perceive that they may receive benefits by doing so.

7. Case, "Discovering the Privilege of Whiteness."

8. Patrick R. Grzanka, Kristen A. Gonzalez, and Lisa B. Spanierman, "White Supremacy and Counseling Psychology: A Critical-Conceptual Framework," *Counseling Psychologist* 49, no. 4 (2019): 478–529.

9. Dorothy E. Roberts, "Racism and Patriarchy in the Meaning of Motherhood," *American University Journal of Gender, Social Policy & the Law* 1, no. 1 (1992): 1–38.

10. Zeus Leonardo, *Race, Whiteness, and Education* (New York: Routledge, 2009).

11. Derald Wing Sue, "Whiteness and Ethnocentric Monoculturalism: Making the 'Invisible' Visible," *American Psychologist* 59, no. 8 (2004): 761–769; Stephanie M. Wildman and Adrienne D. Davis, "Making Systems of Privilege Visible," in *White Privilege: Essential Readings on the Other Side of Racism*, 5th ed., edited by Paula S. Rothenberg (New York: Worth Publishers, 2015): 137–144.

12. Ruth Frankenberg, "Introduction: Local Whitenesses, Localizing Whiteness," in *Displacing Whiteness*, edited by Ruth Frankenberg (Durham, NC: Duke University Press, 1997): 1–34.

13. Whiteness as a concept has a very long social history. Black scholars (W. E. B. DuBois and others) identified Whiteness "as a new religion," one that held the belief that there are racial distinctions and that one race (White) is better than all others. See DuBois, *Souls of Black Folks* (1903). For a short and excellent treatise on the history of Whiteness, see Robert Baird, "The Invention of Whiteness: The Long History of a Dangerous Idea," *The Guardian*, April 20, 2021, https://www.theguardian.com/news/2021/apr/20/the-invention-of-whiteness-long-history-dangerous-idea?CMP=Share_AndroidApp_Other.

14. Zeus Leonardo, ed. *Critical Pedagogy and Race* (Hoboken, NJ: John Wiley & Sons, 2009), 32.

15. Ruth Frankenberg, *White Women, Race Matters: The Social Construction of Whiteness* (Minneapolis: University of Minnesota Press, 1993); Paula S. Rothenberg, *Race, Class, and Gender in the United States: An Integrated Study* (New York: Worth Publishers, 2004). For memoirs of White women antiracism activists, see Mab Segrest, *Memoir of a Race Traitor* (New York: New Press, 1994); Minnie Bruce Pratt, "Identity: Skin Blood Heart," in *Yours in Struggle: Three Feminist Perspectives on Anti-Semitism and Racism*, edited by Ellen Bulkin, Minnie Bruce Pratt, and Barbara Smith (New York: Long Haul Press, 1984), 27–77. See also essayist Adrienne Rich, *Of Woman Born: Motherhood as Experience and Institution* (New York: Bantam Books, 1976).

16. Elizabeth L. W. McKenney, "Reckoning with Ourselves: A Critical Analysis of White Women's Socialization and School Psychology," *School Psychology Review*, September 2021, https://doi.org/10.1080/2372966X.2021.1956856.

17. McKenney, "Reckoning with Ourselves," 12. Ladson-Billings makes a similar point about the lack of inclusivity in the academic curriculum and in the student development theory used by student affairs professionals in higher

education. See Gloria Ladson-Billings, "Just What Is Critical Race Theory and What's It Doing in a Nice Field Like Education?," *International Journal of Qualitative Studies in Education* 11, no. 1 (1998): 7–24.

18. Mimi Schippers, "Recovering the Feminine Other: Masculinity, Femininity, and Gender Hegemony," *Theory and Society* 36, no. 1 (2007): 85–102, 89.

19. Eric Liu, "How to Understand Power," TED-Ed talk, November 2014, https://www.ted.com/talks/eric_liu_how_to_understand_power/transcript?language=en.

20. Crenshaw, quoted in "Intersectional Feminism: What It Means and Why It Matters Right Now," UN Women Newsletter, July 1, 2020, https://www.unwomen.org/en/news/stories/2020/6/explainer-intersectional-feminism-what-it-means-and-why-it-matters.

21. Adrienne Rich, *Blood, Bread, and Poetry: Selected Prose 1979–1985* (New York: W. W. Norton & Company, 1994).

22. In her article "Racism and Patriarchy in the Meaning of Motherhood," Dorothy Roberts analyzes feminism as a theory of power. Quoting Catherine MacKinnon Roberts explains that women's subordination by men forms a system of power relations that is not undercut by women's diversity. She writes: "In this country, which parallels other cultures, women's situation combines unequal pay with allocation to disrespected work, sexual targeting for rape, domestic battering, sexual abuse as children, and systemic sexual harassment; depersonalization, demeaned physical characteristics, use in denigrating entertainment, deprivation of reproductive control, and forced prostitution. To see these practices are done by men to women is to see these abuses as forming a system, a hierarchy of inequality." Mackinnon adds that "bell hooks and many other black feminist scholars reminds us that, 'Patriarchy's ideology, if not its power, is not strictly the domain of white men.' Black men also participate in and gain advantages from patriarchal ideology and power." Catharine A. MacKinnon, "Feminism, Marxism, Method, and the State: Toward Feminist Jurisprudence," *Signs* 8, no. 4 (1983): 635–358, 635.

23. Dominant historical narratives of the modern feminist movement in the US have described White and Black women's activist efforts as completely separate and largely antagonistic during the 1960s and 1970s. But an important finding from sociologist Becky Thompson's 2001 study of white antiracist activists fighting racism during those years revealed that "many white women came to see antiracism racism as a centerpiece of feminism through the activism and writing of women of color" (154). Working closely side by side with Black women and other women of color in the struggle "opened a way for white women to explore how their own multiple identities—class, religion, family, sexuality—might inform their strategies for opposing racism" (154). These women learned to communicate, educate, and support each other across their differences. In her call to action, Thompson implores White women to "look to your own history for signs of heresy and rebellion." That history of resistance exists and has left to Sister Resisters a legacy of cross-racial collaboration

from White antiracism resisters of the past. Becky W. Thompson, *A Promise and a Way of Life: White Antiracist Activism* (Minneapolis: University of Minnesota Press, 2001).

24. Combahee River Collective, "Combahee River Collective Statement," in *Home Girls: A Black Feminist Anthology*, edited by Barbara Smith (New Brunswick: Rutgers University Press, 2000), 264.

25. Ludlow, a White feminist discussing feminism in the classroom, says: "In US culture, the dominant discourse around identity difference is shaped by denial and shame. Many of my white students find it nearly impossible to speak about racial difference; they have been taught that noticing racial differences is rude, that a polite person pretends to live in a color-blind society." Jeannie Ludlow, "From Safe Space to Contested Space in the Feminist Classroom," *Transformations: The Journal of Inclusive Scholarship and Pedagogy* 15, no. 1 (2004): 40–56.

26. Heather Laine Talley, "White Women Doing White Supremacy in Nonprofit Culture," Equity in the Center, September 25, 2019, https://equityinthecenter.org/white-women-doing-white-supremacy-in-nonprofit-culture/.

27. Lyn Mikel Brown and Carol Gilligan, *Meeting at the Crossroads: Women's Psychology and Girls' Development* (New York: Ballantine Books, 1992).

28. Sarah McKibben, "Robin DiAngelo on Educators' 'White Fragility,'" *Educational Leadership* 76, no. 7 (2019), https://www.ascd.org/el/articles/robin-diangelo-on-educators-white-fragility.

29. Robin DiAngelo, "White Fragility," *International Journal of Critical Pedagogy* 3, no. 3 (2011): 54–70.

30. Some White women involved in multiracial coalition building, often within feminist movements, also pushed back against gendered expectations of niceness and docility and White racial blindness. These include progressive Jews, lesbians, and others whose identities engender resistance to the multiple and simultaneous oppressions they faced. See Barbara Smith, Beverly Smith, and Demita Frazier, "A Black Feminist Statement," in *This Bridge Called My Back*, edited by Cherrie Moraga and Gloria Anzaldua (New York: State University of New York Press, 1981), 210–218; Beth Brant, ed., *A Gathering of Spirit: A Collection by North American Indian Women* (Ithaca, NY: Firebrand Books, 1988); Elly Bulkin, Minnie Bruce Pratt, and Barbara Smith, *Yours in Struggle: Three Feminist Perspectives on Anti-Semitism and Racism* (Ithaca NY: Firebrand Books, 1988); Akasha Gloria Hull, Patricia Bell-Scott, and Barbara Smith, eds., *All The Women Are White, All the Blacks Are Men, but Some of Us Are Brave: Black Women's Studies* (New York: Feminist Press, 1982); Becky W. Thompson, *A Promise and a Way of Life: White Anti-racist Activism* (Minneapolis: University of Minnesota Press, 2001).

31. Becky W. Thompson, *A Hunger So Wide and So Deep: American Women Speak Out on Eating Problems* (Minneapolis: University of Minnesota Press, 1994); Charlynn Small and Mazella Fuller, *Treating Black Women with Eating Disorders* (New York: Routledge, 2021); Tamara Beauboeuf-Lafontant, *Behind the Mask of the*

Strong Black Woman: Voice and the Embodiment of a Costly Performance (Philadelphia: Temple University Press, 2009); Tamara Beauboeuf-Lafontant, "Strong and Large Black Women? Exploring Relationships between Deviant Womanhood and Weight," *Gender & Society* 17, no. 1 (2003): 111–121.

32. Talley, "White Women Doing White Supremacy."

33. Claire K. Robbins and Susan R. Jones, "Negotiating Racial Dissonance: White Women's Narratives of Resistance, Engagement, and Transformative Action," *Journal of College Student Development* 57, no. 6 (2016): 633–651.

34. Moya Bailey and Trudy, "On Misogynoir: Citation, Erasure, and Plagiarism," *Feminist Media Studies* 18, no. 4 (2018): 762–768. See also Sabrina Strings, *Fearing the Black Body: The Racial Origins of Fat Phobia* (New York: NYU Press, 2019). In her book on how the female body has been racialized, Strings argues that weight stigma has long been linked with morality and has been used to degrade Black women and discipline White women.

35. See Subini Ancy Annamma, Darrell D. Jackson, and Deb Morrison, "Conceptualizing Color-Evasiveness: Using Dis/ability Critical Race Theory to Expand a Color-Blind Racial Ideology in Education and Society," *Race Ethnicity and Education* 20, no. 2 (2017): 147–162. The authors make a compelling argument regarding the difference between colorblind and color-evasive ideologies.

36. DiAngelo, *White Fragility*, 64.

37. Mary Louise Fellows and Sherene Razack, "The Race to Innocence: Confronting Hierarchical Relations Among Women," *Journal of Gender, Race & Justice* 1 (1997): 335–352.

38. DiAngelo, *White Fragility*, 103.

39. See also Ruby Hamad, *White Tears/Brown Scars: How White Feminism Betrays Women of Colour* (London: Hachette UK, 2020).

40. Christine Tamir, Abby Budiman, Luis Noe-Bustamante, and Lauren Mora, "Facts About the U.S. Black Population," Pew Research Center, March 25, 2021, https://www.pewresearch.org/social-trends/fact-sheet/facts-about-the -us-black-population.

41. Cheryl E. Matias, "Check Yo'self before You Wreck Yo'self and Our Kids: Counterstories from Culturally Responsive White Teachers? . . . To Culturally Responsive White Teachers!," *Interdisciplinary Journal of Teaching and Learning* 3, no. 2 (2013): 68–81.

42. David Roediger, *The Wages of Whiteness: Race and the Making of the American Working Class*, new ed. (New York: Verso, 2007). For more information on how White people became "White," see Noel Ignatiev, *How the Irish Became White* (London: Routledge, 2019); Nell Painter, *The History of White People* (New York: W. W. Norton & Company, 2011).

43. Paul Kivel, "Are You Mentoring for Social Justice?," *Racial Equity Tools* (2004): 129–149, www.paulkivel.com.

44. Peggy McIntosh, "Extending the Knapsack: Using the White Privilege Analysis to Examine Conferred Advantage and Disadvantage," *Women & Therapy* 38, no. 3–4 (2015): 232–245.

45. Maryam M. Jernigan, Carlton E. Green, Leyla Pérez-Gualdrón, Marcia Liu, Kevin T. Henze, Cynthia Chen, Kisha N. Bazelais, Anmol Satiani, Ethan H. Mereish, and Janet E. Helms, #racialtraumaisreal (Chestnut Hill, MA: Institute for the Study and Promotion of Race and Culture, 2015), https://www.bc.edu/content/dam/bc1/schools/lsoe/sites/isprc/racialtraumaisreal.pdf.
46. We'd like to thank Becky Thompson for her assistance with this list.

CHAPTER 3

1. Christopher Ingraham, "Three Quarters of Whites Don't Have Any Non-White Friends," *Washington Post*, August 25, 2014, https://www.washingtonpost.com/news/wonk/wp/2014/08/25/three-quarters-of-whites-dont-have-any-non-white-friends/.
2. Daniel Cox, Juhem Navarro-Rivera, and Robert P. Jones, "Race, Religion, and Political Affiliation of Americans' Core Social Networks," Public Religion Research Institute, August 3, 2016, https://www.prri.org/research/poll-race-religion-politics-americans-social-networks/.
3. Kathy E. Kram, *Mentoring at Work: Developmental Relationships in Organizational Life* (Lanham, MD: University Press of America, 1988); Lisa R. Merriweather and Alberta J. Morgan, "Two Cultures Collide: Bridging the Generation Gap in a Non-traditional Mentorship," *Qualitative Report* 18, no. 12 (2013): 1–16; Linda C. Tillman, "Mentoring African American Faculty in Predominantly White Institutions," *Research in Higher Education* 42, no. 3 (2001): 295–325.
4. Kimberly A. Griffin and Richard J. Reddick, "Surveillance and Sacrifice: Gender Differences in the Mentoring Patterns of Black Professors at Predominantly White Research Universities," *American Educational Research Journal* 48, no. 5 (2011): 1032–1057; Lois A. Benishek, Kathleen J. Bieschke, Jeeseon Park, and Suzanne M. Slattery, "A Multicultural Feminist Model of Mentoring," *Journal of Multicultural Counseling and Development* 32 (2004): 428–442; Denise Goerisch, Jae Basiliere, Ashley Rosener, Kimberly McKee, Jodee Hunt, and Tonya M. Parker, "Mentoring *With*: Reimagining Mentoring Across the University," *Gender, Place & Culture* 26, no. 12 (2019): 1740–1758.
5. Michael J. Nakkula and Sharon M. Ravitch, *Matters of Interpretation: Reciprocal Transformation in Therapeutic and Developmental Relationships with Youth* (San Francisco: Jossey-Bass Publishers, 1998); Michael J. Nakkula and Eric Toshalis, *Understanding Youth: Adolescent Development for Educators* (Cambridge, MA: Harvard Education Press, 2006).
6. Nakkula and Toshalis, *Understanding Youth*.
7. Paul C. Gorski and Noura Erakat, "Racism, Whiteness, and Burnout in Antiracism Movements: How White Racial Justice Activists Elevate Burnout in Racial Justice Activists of Color in the United States," *Ethnicities* 19, no. 5 (2019): 784–808. In their interviews with White racial justice activists, Gorski and Erakat found that White activists attributed their burnout to unresolved racist views, undermining and invalidating the work of activists of color, being unwilling

to take action when needed, exhibiting White fragility, and taking credit for other people's work and ideas.

8. Melanie Tervalon and Jann Murray-García, "Cultural Humility versus Cultural Competence: A Critical Distinction in Defining Physician Training Outcomes in Multicultural Education," *Journal of Health Care for the Poor and Underserved* 9, no. 2 (1998): 117–125; Joshua N. Hook, Don E. Davis, Jesse Owen, Everett L. Worthington, and Shawn O. Utsey, "Cultural Humility: Measuring Openness to Culturally Diverse Clients," *Journal of Counseling Psychology* 60, no. 3 (2013): 353–366.

9. Özlem Sensoy and Robin DiAngelo, "Respect Differences? Challenging the Common Guidelines in Social Justice Education," *Democracy and Education* 22, no. 2 (2014): 1–10, 3. As far back as 1892, Anna Julia Cooper's volume *A Voice from the South* provided an intersectional analysis that precedes both modern Black feminism and what we call *intersectionality* today. Other Black scholars and activists, including W. E. B. DuBois, who argued that the problem of the color line was the primary problem of the twentieth century, similarly challenged mainstream notions about knowledge, race, and power in the early decades of the twentieth century. For a deeper discussion of contemporary intersectionality studies, see Sumi Cho, Kimberlé, Williams Crenshaw, and Leslie McCall, "Toward a Field of Intersectionality Studies: Theory, Applications, and Praxis," *Signs* 38, no. 4 (2013): 785–810.

10. Nordia A. Campbell, "Shifting the Focus: The Role of Institutional and Racial/Ethnic Protective Factors in Promoting Resilience among Black and Latina College Women" (PhD diss., Michigan State University, 2017); Tracy L. Robinson-Wood, "Love, School, and Money: Stress and Cultural Coping among Ethnically Diverse Black College Women: A Mixed-Method Analysis," *Western Journal of Black Studies* 33, no. 2 (2009): 77–86.

11. Campbell, "Shifting the Focus."

12. Patricia Hill Collins, *Black Feminist Thought: Knowledge, Consciousness, and the Politics of Empowerment* (New York: Routledge, 2000).

13. Janie Victoria Ward, "Navigating Inequities: A Morally Rooted Pedagogy of Intentional Mentoring with Black Children and Other Youth of Color," in *Character and Moral Education: A Reader*, edited by Joseph L. DeVitis and Tianlong Yu (New York: Peter Lang, 2011), 295–307.

14. Becky W. Thompson, *A Hunger So Wide and So Deep: American Women Speak Out on Eating Problems* (Minneapolis: University of Minnesota Press, 1994).

15. Collins, *Black Feminist Thought*.

CHAPTER 4

1. Isis H. Settles, Jennifer S. Pratt-Hyatt, and Nicole T. Buchanan, "Through the Lens of Race: Black and White Women's Perceptions of Womanhood," *Psychology of Women Quarterly* 32, no. 4 (2008): 454–468.

2. Tammy L. Henderson, Andrea G. Hunter, and Gladys J. Hildreth, "Outsiders Within the Academy: Strategies for Resistance and Mentoring African American Women," *Michigan Family Review* 14, no. 1 (2010): 28–41, http://dx.doi.org/10.3998/mfr.4919087.0014.105.

3. Monique Morris, *Pushout: The Criminalization of Black Girls in Schools* (New York: New Press, 2016).

4. Jean Baker Miller, *Towards a Psychology of Women* (Boston: Beacon Press, 1976); Mary Field Belenky, Blythe M. Clinchy, Nancy Rule Goldberger, and Jill Mattuck Tarule, *Women's Ways of Knowing: The Development of Self, Voice, and Mind* (New York: Basic Books, 1986); Patricia Hill Collins, *Black Feminist Thought: Knowledge, Consciousness, and the Politics of Empowerment* (New York: Routledge, 2000); Fern L. Johnson and Elizabeth J. Aries, "The Talk of Women Friends," *Women's Studies International Forum* 6, no. 4 (1983): 353–361; Carol Gilligan, *In a Different Voice* (Cambridge, MA: Harvard University Press, 1982). In *Joining the Resistance* (Cambridge: Polity Press, 2011), Gilligan argues that the use of voice, especially when coupled with the capacity to resist false authority and relationship, is needed for both love and for citizenship in today's society.

5. Ana M. Martínez-Alemán, "Race Talks: Undergraduate Women of Color and Female Friendships," *Review of Higher Education* 23, no. 2 (2000): 133–152, 144.

6. Tamara Gilkes Borr, "The Strategic Pursuit of Black Homophily on a Predominantly White Campus," *Journal of Higher Education* 90, no. 2 (2019): 322–346; Miller McPherson, Lynn Smith-Lovin, and James M. Cook, "Birds of a Feather: Homophily in Social Networks," *Annual Review of Sociology* 27, no. 1 (2001): 415–444.

7. Beverly Daniel Tatum, "Family Life and School Experience: Factors in the Racial Identity Development of Black Youth in White Communities," *Journal of Social Issues* 60, no. 1 (2004): 117–135.

8. Discussion of historical and contemporary leadership models among Black women in predominantly White colleges found in Andrea D. Domingue, "'Our Leaders Are Just We Ourself': Black Women College Student Leaders' Experiences with Oppression and Sources of Nourishment on a Predominantly White College Campus," *Equity & Excellence in Education* 48, no. 3 (2015): 454–472.

9. There are four major sororities, all of which were established in the early twentieth century: Alpha Kappa Alpha Sorority (Howard University, 1908), Delta Sigma Theta Sorority (Howard University, 1913), Zeta Phi Beta Sorority (Howard University, 1920), and Sigma Gamma Rho Sorority (Butler University, 1922). These organizations have significantly impacted the African American community, as well as civil society itself. For additional information, see https://www.learningtogive.org/resources/african-american-sororities.

10. Danielle L. Apugo, "'We All We Got': Considering Peer Relationships as Multipurpose Sustainability Outlets Among Millennial Black Women Graduate Students Attending Majority White Urban Universities," *Urban Review* 49, no. 2 (2017): 347–367. See also Danielle L. Apugo, "A Hidden Culture of Coping:

Insights on African American Women's Existence in Predominately White Institutions," *Multicultural Perspectives* 21, no. 1 (2019): 53–62.

11. Quenette L. Walton and Olubunmi Basirat Oyewuwo-Gassikia, "The Case for #BlackGirlMagic: Application of a Strengths-Based, Intersectional Practice Framework for Working with Black Women with Depression," *Affilia* 32, no. 4 (2017): 461–475, 461.

12. Adam Bradley, "The Black Nerds Redefining the Culture," *New York Times*, March 24, 2021, https://www.nytimes.com/2021/03/24/t-magazine/black -nerds-culture.html.

13. Kimberly A. Griffin, Emil L. Cunningham, and Chrystal A. George Mwangi, "Defining Diversity: Ethnic Differences in Black Students' Perceptions of Racial Climate," *Journal of Diversity in Higher Education* 9, no. 1 (2016): 34–49.

14. Tracy Robinson and Janie Victoria Ward, "African American Adolescents and Skin Color," *Journal of Black Psychology* 21, no. 3 (1995): 256–279.

15. Janie Victoria Ward, Tracy L. Robinson-Wood, and Noreen Boadi, "Resisting Everyday Colorism in Schools: Strategies for Identifying and Interrupting the Problem that Won't Go Away," in *Race and Colorism in Education*, edited by Carla R. Monroe (New York: Routledge Press, 2016), 17–35; Margo Okazawa-Rey, Tracy Robinson, and Janie Victoria Ward, "Black Women and the Politics of Skin Color and Hair," *Women & Therapy* 6, no. 1–2 (1987): 89–102.

16. Elizabeth Acevedo, *The Poet X* (New York: HarperCollins, 2018).

17. Julie J. Park, Nida Denson, and Nicholas A. Bowman, "Does Socioeconomic Diversity Make a Difference? Examining the Effects of Racial and Socioeconomic Diversity on the Campus Climate for Diversity," *American Educational Research Journal* 50, no. 3 (2013): 466–496; Patricia Gurin, Eric Dey, Sylvia Hurtado, and Gerald Gurin, "Diversity and Higher Education: Theory and Impact on Educational Outcomes," *Harvard Educational Review* 72, no. 3 (2002): 330–367; Sylvia Hurtado, Alma R. Clayton-Pedersen, Walter Recharde Allen, and Jeffrey F. Milem, "Enhancing Campus Climates for Racial/Ethnic Diversity: Educational Policy and Practice," *Review of Higher Education* 21, no. 3 (1998): 279–302; Shaun R. Harper and Sylvia Hurtado, "Nine Themes in Campus Racial Climates and Implications for Institutional Transformation," *New Directions for Student Services*, no. 120 (2007): 7–24; Ernest T. Pascarella, Mark H. Salisbury, Georgianna L. Martin, and Charles Blaich, "Some Complexities in the Effects of Diversity Experiences on Orientation Toward Social/Political Activism and Political Views in the First Year of College," *Journal of Higher Education* 83, no. 4 (2012): 467–496; Mitchell J. Chang, Alexander W. Astin, and Dongbin Kim, "Cross-racial Interaction Among Undergraduates: Some Consequences, Causes, and Patterns," *Research in Higher Education* 45, no. 5 (2004): 529–553.

18. William Mathis, "Moving Beyond Tracking," Research-Based Options for Education Policymaking, National Education Policy Center, May 2013, https://nepc .colorado.edu/sites/default/files/pb-options-10-tracking.pdf.

19. John Lowe, "Theories of Ethnic Humor: How to Enter, Laughing," *American Quarterly* 38, no. 3 (1986): 439–460, 443.

20. Leon Festinger, *A Theory of Cognitive Dissonance*, vol. 2. (Stanford, CA: Stanford University Press, 1957).

21. Roderick J. Watts, Matthew A. Diemer, and Adam M. Voight, "Critical Consciousness: Current Status and Future Directions," *New Directions for Child and Adolescent Development*, no. 134 (2011): 43–57.

22. Karyn Hall, "Understanding Validation: A Way to Communicate Acceptance," *Psychology Today*, April 26, 2021, https://www.psychology today.com/us/blog/pieces-mind/201204/understanding-validation-way -communicate-acceptance.

CHAPTER 5

1. Gabriella Gutiérrez y Muhs, Yolanda Flores Niemann, Carmen G. González, and Angela P. Harris, ed., *Presumed Incompetent: The Intersections of Race and Class for Women in Academia* (Boulder: University Press of Colorado, 2012).

2. For an extended discussion of the origin of the Karen meme, the history of conflicts between Black and White women in social movements, White women's wrongful convictions of Black men, and other forms of White women's racism, see Helen Lewis, "The Mythology of Karen," *The Atlantic*, August 24, 2020, https://www.theatlantic.com/international/archive/2020/08 /karen-meme-coronavirus/615355/.

3. Historians have well documented animosities between Black and White women in the abolition movement, in which female antislavery societies excluded Black women. White women attendees at the 1851 Women's Rights Convention in Akron, Ohio, begged the conveners to prevent Sojourner Truth's participation. White female suffragettes commonly used Black women when and where they fit White women's goals. See Rosalyn Terborg-Penn, "Discrimination against Afro-American Women in the Woman's Movement, 1830–1920," in *The Afro-American Woman: Struggles and Images*, edited by Sharon Harley and Rosalyn Terborg-Penn (Baltimore: Black Classic Press, 1997), 17–28; Nell Irvin Painter, "Difference, Slavery, and Memory: Sojourner Truth in Feminist Abolitionism," in *The Abolitionist Sisterhood: Women's Political Culture in Antebellum America*, edited by Jean Fagan Yellin and John C. Van Horne (Ithaca, NY: Cornell University Press, 1994), 139–158, 154. Domestic work, one of the few occupations offered to Black women in the pre–civil rights era, brought Black and White women together in physical intimacy within White households, yet White women's racism, their controlling maternalism and infantilization of Black women, was a form of coercion that reinforced the unequal terms of the relationship. See Katherine Van Wormer, David W. Jackson III, and Charletta Sudduth, *The Maid Narratives: Black Domestics and White Families in the Jim Crow South* (Baton Rouge: Louisiana State University Press 2012). See also Judith

Rollins, *Between Women: Domestics and Their Employers* (Philadelphia: Temple University Press, 1985). Finally, Winifred Breines, in her examination of race, class, gender, and sexuality within the Women's Liberation Movement of the 1960s, argues that White women's flawed sense of idealism obscured racial differences between women, rendering Black women's struggles invisible and nonimportant. Winfred Breines, *The Trouble between Us: An Uneasy History of White and Black Women in the Feminist Movement* (Oxford: Oxford University Press, 2006).

4. Christine E. Sleeter, *The Academic and Social Value of Ethnic Studies: A Research Review* (Washington, DC: National Education Association, 2011), https:// vtechworks.lib.vt.edu/bitstream/handle/10919/84024/AcademicSocialValue .pdf?sequence=1&isAllowed=y.

5. Audrey Thompson, "For: Anti-racist Education," *Curriculum Inquiry* 27, no. 1 (1997): 7–44, 15; Carter G. Woodson, *The Mis-education of the Negro* (Washington, DC: Associated Publishers, 1933).

6. Agnes Martin, Noreen Boadi, Caroline Fernandes, Sherry Watt, and Tracy Robinson-Wood, "Applying Resistance Theory to Depression in Black Women," *Journal of Systemic Therapies* 32, no. 1 (2013): 1–13.

7. Resmaa Menakem, *My Grandmother's Hands: Racialized Trauma and the Pathway to Mending Our Hearts and Bodies* (Las Vegas: Central Recovery Press, 2017).

8. Joe Feagin, *Systemic Racism: A Theory of Oppression* (New York: Routledge, 2013).

9. Keon M. McGuire, Saskias Casanova, and Charles H. F. Davis III, "'I'm a Black Female Who Happens to Be Muslim': Multiple Marginalities of an Immigrant Black Muslim Woman on a Predominantly White Campus," *Journal of Negro Education* 85, no. 3 (2016): 316–329; Leila Fadel, "America's Next Generation of Muslims Insists on Crafting its Own Story," April 12, 2018, NPR, *Morning Edition*, https://www.npr.org/2018/04/12/599215203/americas-next-generation -of-muslims-insists-on-crafting-its-own-story; Pew Research Center, "U.S. Muslims Concerned about Their Place in Society, but Continue to Believe in the American Dream," July 26, 2017, https://www.pewforum.org/2017/07/26/findings -from-pew-research-centers-2017-survey-of-us-muslims/.

10. Tammy L. Henderson, Andrea G. Hunter, and Gladys J. Hildreth, "Outsiders Within the Academy: Strategies for Resistance and Mentoring African American Women," *Michigan Family Review* 14, no. 1 (2010), http://dx.doi.org /10.3998/mfr.4919087.0014.105. See also Janie Victoria Ward, "Staying Woke," in *The Crisis of Connection: Roots, Consequences, and Solutions*, edited by Niobe Way, Alisha Ali, Carol Gilligan, and Pedro Noguera (New York: New York University Press, 2018), 106–128.

11. Janet E. Helms, *A Race is a Nice Thing to Have: A Guide to Being a White Person or Understanding the White Persons in Your Life*, 3rd ed. (San Diego: Cognella Academic Publishing, 2018), xiii.

12. Examples of writings from indigenous feminists include Paula Gunn Allen, "Where I Come From Is Like This . . . ," in *Face to Face: Women Writers on Faith, Mysticism, and Awakening*, edited by Linda Hogan and Brenda Peterson (New

York: North Point Press, 2004), 55–62; and Mohja Kahf, "Around the Ka'ba and Over the Crick: A Muslim Girl in Hendricks County," *Religion & Education* 25, no. 1–2 (1998): 38–44.

CHAPTER 6

1. Richard F. Catalano, David J. Hawkins, and John W. Toumbourou, "Positive Youth Development in the United States: History, Efficacy, and Links to Moral and Character Education," in *Handbook of Moral and Character Education*, edited by Larry P. Nucci and Darcia Narvaez (New York: Routledge, 2008): 459–483.

2. Katie Clonan-Roy, Charlotte E. Jacobs, and Michael J. Nakkula, "Towards a Model of Positive Youth Development Specific to Girls of Color: Perspectives on Development, Resilience, and Empowerment," *Gender Issues* 33, no. 2 (2016): 96–121, 115. See also Anita Jones Thomas and Caryn R. R. Rodgers, "Resilience and Protective Factors for African American and Latina Girls," in *Diversity in Mind and in Action*, edited by Jean Lau Chin (Santa Barbara, CA: Praeger, 2009), 117–128.

3. Moya Bailey, "New Terms of Resistance: A Response to Zenzele Isoke," *Souls* 15, no. 4 (2013): 341–343.

4. Carroll Izard, Sarah Fine, David Schultz, Allison Mostow, Brian Ackerman, and Eric Youngstrom, "Emotion Knowledge as a Predictor of Social Behavior and Academic Competence in Children at Risk," *Psychological Science* 12, no. 1 (2001): 18–23. Cited in American Psychological Association, *APA Task Force Report on Resilience and Strength in African American Children and Adolescents* (Washington, DC: American Psychological Association, 2008).

5. Audrey Thompson, "For: Anti-racist Education," *Curriculum Inquiry* 27, no. 1 (1997): 7–44.

6. Howard C. Stevenson, *Promoting Racial Literacy in Schools: Differences that Make a Difference* (New York: Teachers College Press, 2014). 115.

7. Stevenson, *Promoting Racial Literacy in Schools*, 18.

8. Breonna Taylor was a twenty-six-year-old Black woman who was fatally shot in her Louisville, Kentucky, apartment by plainclothes police. The officers forced entry into her apartment, purportedly while investigating drug dealings. Questions remain about the raid. Whether police announced themselves before entry remains under dispute, and more than a year after Breonna died, no police had been charged in Taylor's death. Her death sparked outrage and massive demonstrations across the nation against overpolicing and criminal injustice in Black communities.

9. Erik H. Erikson, *Identity: Youth and Crisis* (New York: W. W. Norton & Company, 1968).

10. Monica T. Williams, Isha W. Metzger, Chris Leins, and Celenia DeLapp, "Assessing Racial Trauma Within a DSM-5 Framework: The UConn Racial/Ethnic Stress & Trauma Survey," *Practice Innovations* 3, no. 4 (2018): 242–260.

11. Greta Anderson, "The Emotional Toll of Racism," Inside Higher Ed, October 23, 2020, https://www.insidehighered.com/news/2020/10/23/racism-fuels-poor -mental-health-outcomes-black-students; Lynya Floyd, "Black Women Are Facing an Overwhelming Mental Health Crisis," *Prevention*, November 6, 2020; Inger Burnett-Zeigler, *Nobody Knows the Trouble I've Seen: The Emotional Lives of Black Women* (New York: Amistad, 2021).

12. Della V. Mosley, Candice N. Hargons, Carolyn Meiller, Blanka Angyal, Paris Wheeler, Candice Davis, and Danelle Stevens-Watkins, "Critical Conscious-ness of Anti-Black Racism: A Practical Model to Prevent and Resist Racial Trauma," *Journal of Counseling Psychology* 68, no. 1 (2021): 1–16.

13. Layla F. Saad, *Me and White Supremacy: Combat Racism, Change the World, and Become a Good Ancestor* (Naperville, IL: Sourcebooks, 2020).

14. Greta Anderson, "The Emotional Toll of Racism," *Inside Higher Ed*, October 23, 2020.

15. Fernanda Zamudio-Suarez, "Race on Campus," *Chronicle of Higher Education*, January 12, 2021, https://www.chronicle.com/newsletter/race-on-campus /2021-01-12.

16. Audre Lorde, *A Burst of Light: And Other Essays* (Ithaca, NY: Firebrand Books, 1988).

ACKNOWLEDGMENTS

N EARLY FORTY YEARS AGO, Tracy and I met as graduate students at Harvard University. We began with a publication of our theory of resistance thirty years ago, and we have been writing together ever since. We are thankful for the sisterhood that we share. Over the years, we have discussed the importance of a mentoring practice that is relevant for Black female college students and are proud to present here what we have learned. We appreciate our families and friends who, for years, have lovingly prodded, "How is that book coming along?" Our angel parents abide with us, and their wisdom continues to illuminate our paths. We hold them in our hearts forever. We thank Caroline Chauncey at Harvard Education Press for her early and insightful support in shaping the theme of this book. We especially appreciate our editor Jayne Fargnoli, whose encouragement, excitement, and genuine interest in our Sister Resister model has cheered us on at every turn. The conversations between us strengthened our writing and her devotion to this work fortified our passion. Great books do not get to press without great editors. Thank you, Jayne, for the optimism, critical eye, and extreme kindness that you brought to this project.

Our students Chantal Muse, Jaylan Abd Elrahman, and Halley Jeremie have guided us with their wisdom, research acumen, technical support, and invaluable insights. We are enormously grateful for their contributions over the years. We owe a huge dose of gratitude to the many undergraduate and graduate students and research participants who took part in our research studies, focus groups, one-on-one interviews, surveys, and senior internships. We hope that we have lifted up your voices with the loving care and respect that they deserve. Many thanks to the colleagues and wise women who have walked with us at various stages of this journey: Marilyn and Claudia Barber, Oyenike Balogun-Mwangi, Bithia Carter, Karen T. Craddock, Miriam Diamond, Rita Smith Dove, Ivy George, Jessica Parr, Karen Spikes, and Sherry Kay Watt. Beginning in graduate school, Ann Early Clyde has been my (Tracy) treasured friend and peer mentor and has graciously championed me and this work. I love and honor our friendship. We want to thank our Sistah friend and colleague Becky Thompson for her thoughtful and reflective feedback on early drafts of this manuscript. As a consummate Sister Resister, her knowledge of White antiracist activism was invaluable, and we appreciate her assistance in strengthening our work. And to my dear friend Alyssa Walker, thank you for your listening ear and heart in developing the framework of resistance for White women.

Janie: To my family, Eli and Judy, and to my beloved community of friends, Linda and the Cohens, Kat and the Tennermanns—I couldn't have finished this book without the humor, encouragement, moral support, and constant strength that you always offered me throughout the years. My love for you all is deep and unending. Thank you.

Tracy: My children are my light and life, and Geoffrey's love sustains me. My family has encouraged me to rise, to shine, to say what I need to say, and to boldly write this book. I am grateful in ways that words cannot express.

Tracy: I want to thank you from the bottom of my heart, Janie Ward, for asking me to join you in the writing of this book. You are my sister and I love you very much. *Janie:* And I want to thank you, Tracy Robinson-Wood, for saying yes to my invitation, for following through even in the tough times, and for always being there when it counts. I love you forever.

ABOUT THE AUTHORS

Janie Victoria Ward is professor emerita in the Departments of Education and Africana Studies at Simmons University in Boston, Massachusetts. She holds a master's degree in counseling and consulting psychology and a doctorate in human development from Harvard Graduate School of Education.

Ward is a coeditor of *Mapping the Moral Domain: A Contribution of Women's Thinking to Psychological Theory and Research* (Harvard University Press, 1988) with Carol Gilligan. With Tracy L. Robinson, Ward coedited a compilation of sixteen autobiographical statements written by African American, Caribbean, and Black Canadian college students entitled *Souls Looking Back: Life Stories of Growing Up Black* (Routledge, 1999). Ward's book *The Skin We're In: Teaching Our Children to be Emotionally Strong, Socially Smart and Spiritually Connected* (Fireside, 2000) focused on racial socialization in Black families.

For over thirty years, her professional work and research interests have centered on the developmental issues of African American adolescents, focusing on identity and moral development in African American girls and boys. Professor Ward continues to work with youth counselors, secondary school educators, college staff, and other practitioners in a variety of settings.

Dr. Tracy Robinson-Wood is a professor of applied psychology at Northeastern University. Her research explores intersectionality and psychosocial identity. She and her intersectionality research team have examined microaggressions among highly educated BIPOC and White people who identify as LGBTQ, racial socialization messages among adult biracial people, and the psychological impact of viewing videos of interactions between police and civilians. The fifth edition of her textbook *The Convergence of Race, Ethnicity, and Gender: Multiple Identities in Counseling* was published in 2017.

A native of Sacramento, California, Dr. Robinson-Wood earned her bachelor of arts in psychology and communication arts from Azusa Pacific University in Azusa, California. Her EdM and EdD are in human development and psychology from the Harvard Graduate School of Education. Dr. Robinson-Wood is a certified EMDR therapist and a licensed clinician both in Massachusetts and in New Hampshire. She resides with her husband, twin daughters, and lovebirds in NH.

INDEX